FROM HUMOR TO INSPIRATION

Jokes, Reflections and Quotes to Enliven Your Day

Ron W.,

Best wishes for an inspired life.

Fr. Mathew Vellankal

Fr. Mathew Vellankal

Holy Spirit Church
37588 Fremont Blvd,
Fremont, CA

DEDICATED TO

The Salesians of Don Bosco, especially of the Province of
Guwahati, India, with whom I learned the importance of joy
and laughter.

CONTENTS

ACKNOWLEDGEMENT

Thank you first to Most Reverent Michael C. Barber SJ, Bishop of Oakland for the Foreword to the book. I am extremely grateful to Dr. Fr. George Plathottam SDB for meticulously reading the draft and making valuable suggestions. Sincere appreciation to Ted and Denise Foster for copy editing. Thank you Lalu Paul for your constant encouragement and technical support. Many thanks to Charissa Rosario, an 8th grade student of Holy Spirit School, Fremont, for the illustrations.

FOREWORD

In **From Humor to Inspiration,** noted pastor and speaker Father Mathew Vellankal has written a rare blend of laughter-inducing jokes and soul-searching reflections. Humor is the best antidote to boredom. Good public speakers use jokes and humorous anecdotes to enliven their speech and engage their audience. Humor is a great leveler-- it cuts through class, status, position or other ranks. Ability to laugh at the funny stories and trifles about others will help us also to laugh at our own foibles and mistakes, to rid ourselves of our false ego. Humor can help remove anxiety and tension. I would say a chuckle in time can save you a few wrinkles on your forehead; a hearty laugh might help ward off even a heart attack!

From Humor to Inspiration takes you beyond mere lung-splitting laughter. It leads you to ponder on the more precious values that guide our life. The inspirational messages and thought provoking reflections, apt quotations from Scriptures and pithy sayings in the book help one to look at life with a totally new perspective.

The book is undoubtedly an invaluable companion for everyone, but more particularly for public speakers, political and civic leaders, religious preachers, teachers and others in leadership positions.

And now get on! Have a hearty laugh. And don't forget to take a moment to ponder your journey in life as well.

Most Reverend Michael C. Barber, SJ
Bishop of Oakland

INTRODUCTION

Teihard de Chardin says: "Joy is the most infallible sign of the presence of God." Jesus used stories and parables to inspire and illustrate his message. Someone has aptly said "Jesus spells Joy". Though we do not see too many pictures of Jesus smiling, he certainly had a great sense of humor and could be funny at times. Remember the passage about taking out the log from your eyes before you take out a splinter from your neighbor's eyes, or the image of a camel going through the eye of a needle! One can visualize Jesus' listeners laughing with this hyperbole and other humor.

The jokes in this book have been gathered over several years from different sources -- conversations, friends, books and magazines. They come from the imagination of many creative people. They have helped me to cheer up and lighten many moments, foster friendship and build fellowship in communities. They have served to make my presentations and homilies interesting and thought provoking. In fact, I have rarely given a Sunday homily or conducted a presentation without at least once making my listeners laugh. Once people have a hearty laugh, they are more disposed to listen to me. They become more attentive and receptive to the message.

These jokes, reflections and quotes, I believe, are timeless; they are appropriate for all age groups. You can read just one joke a day with the reflections and quotes that follow and laugh or smile and think about it throughout the day. Alternatively, you can read the book from cover to cover and just sit back and enjoy its contents. It can lighten and enliven your day and leave you inspired.

The CONTENTS at the beginning, the themes given at the end of the reflections and the INDEX at the end of this book will help you to find the most appropriate joke that suits particular occasions.

I have added for each joke relevant illustrations and quotes so that in addition to having a good laugh, you can draw valuable messages for life. So the purpose of the book is to seek new meaning and purpose in our daily living. It is my hope that this book will give you much joy, inspiration and lead you to experience the divine. By sharing these jokes in our conversations, you can also cheer up others and bring joy into their lives.

The short reflections are connected with the theme of the joke. The quotes offered with every joke enhance the topic. The book can serve as a handy travelling companion, and help one pass time and feel relaxed. After all, you don't need much concentration to relish the contents of the book. It is my hope that the book will be particularly useful for preachers, public speakers, teachers, and animators.

People love persons who have senses of humor. Even if you do not have a natural sense of humor, this book will assist you to develop one. After reading through this book, select a few that you like best. Read them over and over and start telling them to your family and friends.

I have heard people telling me: "I love your jokes but can't remember them." This book help you to solve that problem. Place bookmarks on those jokes that you like most and read them before you go to a party. Then try cracking one or two of your favorites. You will have people explode in wholehearted laughter and you will always remember those jokes.

Laughter is the best medicine not only for the body but also for the brain and memory. According to Nicolas-Sebastien Chambord, "If taking vitamins doesn't keep you healthy enough, try more laughter. The most wasted of all days is that on which one has not laughed." I do not want to hold you up. Go ahead, enjoy the jokes, have a hearty laugh. Live a joyous and healthy life.

Fr. Mathew Vellankal

1. GOD MADE YOU

Little Johnny sitting on the lap of grandpa and feeling the wrinkles on his face, asks him: "Grandpa, did God make you?

Grandpa replies: "Yes, God made me."

Johnny, feeling his own smooth face, asks again: "Grandpa, tell me, did God make me also?"

Grandpa: "Of course, God did. Why do you ask?"

Johnny: "Don't you think that God is doing a better job nowadays?"

* * *

God does a great job with His creation. You are His masterpiece. You are the crown of his creation. You are made in his own image and likeness. You are so very unique and there is only one *you* in the whole world. You are so very precious to Him and He loves you with an everlasting love.

What makes you different makes you beautiful. Embrace that uniqueness and be true to yourself. Do not spend time comparing yourself with others.

"Can a mother forget her infant, be without tenderness for the child of her womb? Even should she forget, I will never forget you. See, upon the palms of my hand I have engraved you." (Isaiah 49: 15-16)

"To be yourself in a world that is constantly trying to make you someone else is the greatest accomplishment." – Ralph Waldo Emerson

Themes: God, Grandpa, Grandson, Maker, Creation, Uniqueness, Masterpiece, Mother, Accomplishment.

2. OBEDIENT SPOUSE

According to a story everyone had died and gone to heaven. God the Father met everyone and told the men to take one side and women the other side.

Then he told the men to make two lines. The first line of those who controlled their wives and the second line of those who were controlled by their wives.

In the first line there was only one man standing, while the second line was miles and miles long. So God the Father walked up to the only man on the first line and said to him: "Congratulations! Tell all those men how you controlled your wife."

Then he replied: "God the Father, I don't know why I am standing here! My wife told me to stand here."

* * *

Marriage is a relationship that two people enter into. In that relationship, mutual respect and esteem are vital. It is not a question of controlling or dominating. The two have to become good friends where they experience profound love.

Have something positive to say to each other daily. Show genuine appreciation for each other everyday. Above all, bring abundance of forgiveness to your family life. Never go to sleep with anger or hatred.

Marriage is when two people become one, but the problem starts when they try to decide which one. A good marriage is not just about marrying the right person; it is also about being the right person.

"Happy marriage is the union of two good forgivers." – Ruth Bell Graham

"Motto for the bride and groom: We are a work in progress with a lifetime contract." – Phyllis Koss

Themes: Obedience, Marriage, Husband, Wife, Men, Women, God, Control, Equality, Respect, Love, Forgiveness, Sharing.

3. LEAD BY EXAMPLE

A four-year-old daughter was watching her mother cook. Then she noticed that her mother had few streaks of gray hair. " Mom," she asked: "why are some of your hairs gray?"

The Mom thought that to be an opportunity to admonish her daughter. So she said: "Each time you do a mischief, one of my hairs turn gray."

Without missing a beat, the little girl asked: "Then why is grandma's hair all gray?"

* * *

Good example is better than preaching or advice because it has far- reaching influence. Try to be an example to others by living authentic lives. Then others will imitate you and they also will become good examples.

Your actions should be consistent with your words. Parents have to remember that one day their children will follow their example instead of their advice.

"My life is my message." – Mahatma Gandhi

"Preach at all times, use words if necessary." – St. Francis of Assisi

Themes: Good Example, Message, Life, Actions, Preaching, Advice, Authenticity.

4. GOD WATCHES

This happened in a convent school cafeteria. Children were lining up for their lunch. At the beginning of the table there was a tray of apples and a nun had placed a note: "Take only one, God is watching."

At the end of the table there was a tray of chocolate chip cookies. One naughty kid placed a note there that read: "Take all you want, God is watching the apples."

* * *

You are the apple of God's eye. God watches over you with great love. He loves you so much that He doesn't want to take His eyes off you. Since God sees you all the time, you have to do the right thing and be pleasing to God.

No matter what you have done or where you have been, God's love is unconditional. He totally forgives your wrongdoing or the mess you have made. God will never give up on you. You are loved by God and nothing can take His love away from you.

"God loves each of us as if there were only one of us." – St. Augustine

"Though our feelings come and go, His love for us does not." – C. S. Lewis

Themes: God, Love, Children, Forgiveness, School, Convent, Watching.

5. A MOTHER'S LESSON

A mother was preparing pancakes and her two sons, Ryan, aged 5, and Kevin, aged 3, were fighting about who should have the first pancake. The mother thought to be an occasion to teach them a moral lesson. She said: "If Jesus were here, He would say: 'Let my brother have the first pancake.'"

Ryan turns to Kevin and said: "Kevin, you be Jesus now."

* * *

Being Christ-like means putting on Christ-like attitudes and behavior. You have to be loving, forgiving and treating the others as if they were your own brothers and sisters. See the face of Christ in everyone you encounter.

Do random acts of kindness every day. One kind word can change someone's entire day. Ask yourself in every circumstance: "What would Jesus do?'

"Because God has made us for Himself, our hearts are restless until they rest in Him." – St. Augustine of Hippo

"The king will say to them in reply, 'Amen, I say to you, whatever you did for one of these least of the brothers of mine, you did it for me.'" – Matthew 25:40

Themes: Christ-like, Jesus, Imitation, Golden Rule, Love, Forgiveness, Mother, Children, Lesson.

6. The Pastor and the Bus Driver

An old pastor and a bus driver died and reached the pearly gates at the same time. As soon as St. Peter saw them, he warmly welcomed the bus driver inside. The pastor was made to stand in the cold, outside the gate for a long time. St. Peter escorted the driver and showed him his beautiful chamber.

After a long time, St. Peter returned to talk to the pastor. The pastor was very furious and said: "I have been a good pastor for a very long time and I have served the Lord very faithfully. Is this the treatment that you give me? Why did you give so much importance to that bus driver and not to me?"

St. Peter replied: "There is a difference. When you preached, everyone slept but when the bus driver drove the bus, everyone prayed."

* * *

Prayer is communication with God. It is a two-way conversation between you and God. That entails talking and listening and spending quality time in His presence. If you believe that God is your best friend, then this conversation becomes easy.

Start your prayer by thanking God for all the blessings that you have received. Then ask for forgiveness for the offenses you have committed. Finally, tell Him your needs. Visualize what you are praying for.

One essential aspect of prayer is faith. When you pray in faith, your intentions will be granted, for Christ has assured: "Ask and you shall receive." When you pray in faith impossible things become possible. Pray as if everything depends on God and work as if everything depends on you.

"Seven days without prayer makes one weak." – Allen E. Vartlett

"Prayer does not change God, but it changes him who prays." – Soren Kierkegaard

Themes: Prayer, Sleep, Pastor, Preacher, Priest, Heaven, Pearly Gate, Peter, Driver, God, Lord.

7. PROBLEM OF EMPTINESS

A mother and her four-year daughter Vanessa had been to church for morning service. While they were returning, Vanessa complained that her stomach was paining. "It is because your stomach is empty," said the mother, "you will feel much better if you had something inside."

That evening the pastor of their church was visiting the family and having dinner with them. As soon as he arrived, he said, "I have been having a headache the whole day."

Little Vanessa immediately said, "That is because your head is empty. You will feel much better if you had something inside."

* * *

You have to empty yourself if you need to receive more. Self-emptying helps to hold whatever is important for you.

If you do not have a goal or vision in life, you could live a meaningless, empty life. People search for pleasures because they feel the emptiness of their lives.

Be careful of what you are feeding your mind. Read things that uplift you, listen to things that inspire you and watch things that motivate you.

"Life is like a flute ... it may have many holes and emptiness. But if you work on it carefully it can play magical melodies." – Anonymous

"The most beautiful things in life cannot be seen or even touched, they must be felt with the heart." – Helen Keller

Themes: Emptiness, Void, Mother, Child, Pastor, Priest, Church, Family, Pain, Ache, Interior, Fullness.

8. FIND THE TRUTH

An elementary school teacher was teaching second graders about marine animals and said: "The whales, even though they are very large, have throats that are comparatively very small."

A little girl put up the hand and said, "That is not true. We read in the Bible that Jonah was swallowed by a whale."

The teacher replied: "That cannot be true."

The girl said, "I am going to ask Jonah about it when I go to heaven."

The teacher asked, "What will you do if he is in hell?"

The girl retorted: "Then you ask him."

* * *

Teaching is a noble profession. A teacher helps to shape the future by shaping the minds of students. A teacher's job is to bring out the best in the students and prepare them for the life ahead. Give importance to the development of imagination in the pupil.

No one can take away from you the wisdom and learning you have gained. Any knowledge gained will be useful someday.

You can learn from the cradle to the grave. Learn from mistakes, remain curious and keep learning. Never say that you have arrived and stop learning, because life never stops teaching. Whether you are young or old, you have someone to learn from.

"Education is the most powerful weapon we can use to change the world." – Nelson Mandela

"Education is not the learning of facts, but the training of the mind to think." – Albert Einstein

Themes: Teacher, Education, Learning, Knowledge, Wisdom, Intelligence, Science, Heaven, Hell, Girl, Faith.

9. GREATEST PERSON

A teacher in the second grade class: "Who is the greatest person ever lived? If you give me the correct answer, you will get $10.00.

An Irish boy put the hand up said: "It is St. Patrick." The teacher said: "no".

A Scottish girl said: "It is St. James." "No", said the teacher.

A Jewish boy said: "It is Jesus Christ." "Correct," said the teacher, "come and get your reward."

As the boy came to the desk of the teacher, she whispered: "Being Jewish, I thought you would say Moses."

The Jewish boy replied: "Yes, in my heart I know it is Moses, but business is business!"

* * *

For Christians the most significant figure in history is Jesus Christ. He tops the list of world's top ten most significant people ever according to Wikipedia.

How do you measure someone's greatness? According to H.G. Wells, an historian: "A man's greatness can be measured by what he leaves to grow, and whether he started others to think along fresh lines with a vigor that persisted after." By this test Jesus stands first.

"I have read in Plato and Cicero sayings that are very wise and very beautiful; but I never read in either of them: Come unto me all ye that labor and are heavy laden." – St. Augustine

"Alexander, Caesar, Charlemagne, and I have founded empires. But on what did we rest the creations of our genius? Upon force. Jesus Christ founded his empire upon love; and at this hour millions of men would die for him." – Napoleon Bonaparte

Themes: Greatest, Teacher, Student, Pupil, Business, Reward, Jesus Christ, Moses, St. Patrick, Christians.

10. MEMORIALS IN THE CHURCH

After the Sunday service, the five-year-old Jeff noticed that there was a plaque with names of people at the entrance of the church. "Pastor, who are all these people?" Jeff asked.

"These are people who died during service," replied the pastor.

Jeff asked: "Which service, at the 9:00 a.m. or the 11:00 a.m.?

* * *

When you give selflessly of your time, talent or treasure for others, you receive much in return. There is much joy in giving than receiving.

The Dead Sea is dead, because no water flows out of it. You will be dead too, if nothing flows out from you to others.

The Bible says that what you do to the least of your brothers and sisters, you do to Jesus himself. Jesus says that your salvation depends on the how much you care for your brothers and sisters by feeding the hungry, giving water to the thirsty, clothing the naked, and visiting the prison.

"Even after all this time, the sun never says to the earth 'you owe me.' Look what happens with a love like that. It lights the whole sky." – Hafiz of Persia

"We can't help everyone, but everyone can help someone." – Dr. Loretta Scott

Themes: Service, Giving, Charity, Selfless giving, Sacrifice, Death, Love, Salvation, Bible, Jesus.

11. SILENCE IN THE CHURCH

Teacher during the catechism class to the first graders: "Why is it necessary to be silent in the church?"

One of the students, Denise, lifted her hand and said: "Because there are people sleeping there."

* * *

The Vatican II documents say that your participation at the Eucharist should be full, conscious and active. Full means you come on time and you do not leave until the Mass is over. Conscious would mean that you are aware and alert to what is taking place during the entire liturgy. You can be active by taking part whole-heartedly in the singing and prayers.

The Holy Mass is the greatest prayer and the Eucharistic sacrifice is the supreme act of worship. Plan your day in such a way that you can spend quality time with the God we worship and not be in a hurry to depart. God deserves your best.

It is in silence, that you hear the voice of God. Do not just babble a lot of prayers, but take time to listen to God speak to you.

"This is the wonderful truth, my dear friends: the Word, which became flesh two thousand years ago, is present today in the Eucharist." – St. John Paul II

"Do you want our Lord to give you many graces? Visit Him often."

– St. John Bosco

Themes: Holy Mass, Eucharist, Sacrifice, Silence, Listening, Worship, Prayer Sleep, Participation.

12. Job Compromise

Jack, the painter, often would thin his paint by adding some turpentine. So when the church decided to paint the roof, Jack gave the lowest bid and got the job. As always, he thinned his paint way down with turpentine.

One day while he was up on the roof – the job almost completed – he heard a loud clap of thunder in the sky. There was another thunder and a heavy shower. With that Jack fell off the roof and all the paint was being washed down.

So Jack looked up to the heavens and prayed: "O Lord, what have you done? I am so very sorry. What should I do?"

And from the thunder, he heard a mighty voice: "Repaint, repaint! And thin no more!"

* * *

There are temptations all around you and you can be a victim to them very easily. The Bible says that even a just person sins seven times a day. But you can take a U-turn and have a change of heart and mind. To repent means to change the direction of one's life. Take responsibility for your wrong doings and admit your failures. Repentance and confession of your sins are important for receiving forgiveness from God and for your peace with God.

You will be serene and peaceful if you are at peace with God and your neighbor. Do not unnecessarily carry the burden of guilt. Learn to let go of the past mistakes and failures.

"God's will is to save us, and nothing pleases him more than our coming back to him with true repentance." – St. Maximus the Confessor

God has promised forgiveness to your repentance, but he has not promised tomorrow to your procrastination." – St. Augustine

Themes: Repentance, Sin, Conversion, Sin, Transformation, Contrition, Penance, Confession, Reconciliation, Forgiveness, Lent.

13. THE DEAL TO DRIVE

Jeremy had just gotten his driving permit. He asked his father, who was a minister, if they could discuss his use of the car.

The Reverend said to him, "I'll make a deal with you. You bring your grades up, study your Bible a little, and get your hair cut, then we will talk about it."

A month later Jeremy came back and again asked his father if they could discuss his use of the car.

His father said, "Son, I'm real proud of you. You have brought your grades up, you've studied your Bible diligently, but you didn't get your hair cut!"

Jeremy waited a moment and replied, "You know Dad, I've been thinking about that. You know Samson had long hair, Moses had long hair, Noah had long hair, and even Jesus had long hair."

His father replied, "Yes Jeremy, and they walked everywhere they went!"

* * *

Change is difficult but the reward is great. Making a lasting change in behavior is a tedious process involving effort and time. There is no single solution that works for everyone. Have clear goals and unflinching motivation.

Your beliefs don't make you a better person; your behavior does. Your thoughts influence your life far beyond you know. Your behavior decides who will stay in your life.

"It's better to hang out with people who are better than you. Pick out associates whose behavior is better than yours and you'll drift in that direction." – Warren Buffett

"Everyone thinks of changing the world, but no one thinks of changing himself." – Leo Tolstoy

Themes: Bible, Father, Son, Samson, Moses, Jesus, Driving, Walking, Behavior Change, Conversion, Transformation.

14. CONDEMNATION OF ALL PARISHIONERS

A pastor had a bad night and in the morning he got onto the pulpit and started his homily by saying: "I say everyone in this parish will go to hell!"

There was a man sitting at the back pew, who was laughing away. So the priest repeated louder, "I say everyone in this parish will go to hell!"

The guy at the back of the church still continued to laugh away. So the pastor walked up to him and asked, "Why are you laughing?"

He replied, "Father, it is because I am not from this parish."

* * *

You do not belong to a parish, a city, a country or the earth forever. Your life on this planet is only a temporary assignment. At the end of your life, you will leave your world to enter into the realm of angels and saints. You belong to heaven and that is where your permanent citizenship is.

Your life here on earth is preparation for the next. When you live in the light of eternity your values change. Think of your destiny daily and live a committed life because you are made to last forever.

"Surely God would not have created such a being as man to exist only for a day! No, no. Man was made for immortality." – Abraham Lincoln

"Love is our true destiny. We do not find the meaning of life by ourselves alone – we find it with another." – Thomas Merton

Themes: Parish, Parishioner, Condemnation, Pastor, Priest, Heaven, Hell, Laughter, Church, Father, Immortality, Eternity.

15. UNDISCIPLINED BROTHERS

Matt, who's seven and his brother Mark, who's five, were very naughty boys. They were often found doing mischief. One day their mother went to the pastor and requested if he would discipline her two boys.

The pastor told her to send the boys one by one to him starting with the older one.

As soon as Matt entered the office, the pastor asked him sternly, "Where is God?" Matt kept silent. The pastor asked him again. No response. So the pastor yelled at him, and asked a third time, "Where is God?" At that point, Matt darted out of the office and went home and hid himself in a closet.

Now Mark knocked on the closet and asked Matt: "Hi, tell me, what happened? " Matt: "We are in deep trouble! God is missing, and they think that we are responsible."

* * *

God is very close to you and is never missing. If you are far away from Him, God may seem distant. The Bible says that when you draw closer to God, He will come closer to you. You may feel lost and alone, but God knows exactly where you are, and He has a good plan for your life.

God dwells in your heart and so don't search for him in the sky. He is everywhere within you and in your brothers and sisters.

Put God first, and all other things will fall into their proper place.

"God gave us the gift of life; it is up to us to give ourselves the gift of living well." – Voltaire

God gave you a heart to love with, not to hate with. God gave you the ability to create heaven on earth, not hell." – Leon Brown

Themes: God, Sunday, Pastor, Parish, Parish Priest, Discipline, Mother, Mischief, Responsibility.

16. Until Death Do Us Part

A few months after their marriage a couple were sitting in the living room relaxing.

Wife asked, "What are you reading?"

Husband shrugged and said, "Nothing."

Wife insisted, "I see that you are reading the marriage certificate."

Husband admitted, "Yes, I'm trying to locate the expiry date."

* * *

There is no expiry date on your marriage certificate. The marriage vows say, "Until death do us part." It is an unbreakable bond that you enter into and so you have to do it with serious thought and reflection. It takes hard work on the part of both of the couple to make marriage work.

A wedding is a day; a marriage is a lifetime. A perfect

marriage is two imperfect people who refuse to give up on each other.

"The willingness to take responsibility for somebody other than yourself is at the root of every successful marriage." – L. Ron Hubbard

"To keep your marriage brimming, with love in the loving cup, whenever you're wrong, admit it; whenever you're right, shut up." – Ogden Nash

Themes: Marriage, Wedding, Nuptial, Matrimony, Vows, Certificate, Husband, Wife, Commitment.

17. THE PROBLEM OF THE PASTORS

Three pastors met together to discuss their common problem. Pigeons were making nests in the churches and were cooing during the services causing disturbances.

The Baptist pastor said, I tried poisoning them and they still come back."

The Presbyterian pastor said, "I tried to electrocute them but they still come back."

The Catholic pastor said, "You know, I did something special and they do not come back often."

"What did you do?" asked the other two pastors in unison.

"Well, I baptized them," said the Catholic pastor, "and they come back only for Christmas and Easter!"

* * *

Baptism is a sacrament of initiation to faith. Through this sacrament you are officially received into the church. It is the joyous beginning of a lifetime of loving and serving the Lord.

The stain of original sin is washed away through baptism. The person baptized becomes officially a member of the Church. He or she is incorporated into the mystical body of Christ. As members of the Church, you have certain rights and duties. Know them and fulfill them. Keep the flame of faith alive in your hearts.

"The faithful are born anew by Baptism, strengthened by the sacrament of Confirmation, and receive in the Eucharist the food of eternal life."

– Pope Paul VI

"All the baptized must announce Jesus with our life, with our witness and with our words." – Pope Francis

Themes: Pastor, Church, Catholic, Baptist, Presbyterian, Disturbance, Baptism, Christening, Sacraments, Christmas, Easter.

18. BLAMING OTHERS

A Catholic priest was invited to celebrate Mass in the neighboring parish church as the pastor there was away on vacation. The priest started the Mass, "In the name of the Father, and of the Son and of the Holy Spirit."

Then he realized that his microphone was not working and so he tapped on his lapel microphone and said, "There is something wrong with the mike."

And the congregation replied, "And also with your spirit!"

* * *

People often tend to see what is wrong with others and fail to see their own mistakes and failures. Look for the good in others and appreciate them as often as you can. Avoid focusing on the failures of others.

Remember when you point a finger at another there are three fingers that are pointing towards you.

When you are offended at any man's fault, turn to yourself and study your own failings. Then you will forget your anger." – Epictetus

"The best years of your life are the ones in which you decide your problems are your own. You do not blame them on your mother, the ecology, or the president. You realize that you control your own destiny." – Albert Ellis

Themes: Problems, Mistakes, Errors, Faults, Failures, Sins, Accusation, Blame.

19. EXPENSIVE FUNERAL

A man went from the United States with his mother-in-law to the Holy Land in Israel with a group of pilgrims. While they were there, the mother-in-law had a heart attack and died. So he went to the undertaker to make funeral arrangements.

The funeral director said, "You have two options. We can

bury her body here for $500. or ship her body to the United States, which will cost you $5,000.

The man replied, "I prefer that you ship her to the U.S."

The funeral director asked again, "Why spend so much money when we can bury her for one tenth of the cost?"

The man said, "You see, two thousand years ago they buried a guy here and after three days he rose to life! I don't want to take chances."

* * *

The resurrection of Jesus was the central theme of the preaching of the apostles. "If Jesus has not risen from death, our preaching is in vain, and your faith is futile and you are still in sins. (1 Corinthians 15: 14) The resurrection of Christ is the basis of Christian faith.

Each time you fall and you get up, you participate in the power of resurrection. Each time you love again after having your love rejected, you participate in the power of resurrection. Each time you fail and try again, you participate in the power of resurrection.

"We are an Easter people, Alleluia is our song." – St. Augustine of Hippo

"Outside of the cross of Jesus Christ, there is no hope in this world. That cross and resurrection at the core of the Gospel is the only hope for humanity. Wherever you go, ask God for wisdom on how to get that Gospel in, even in the toughest situations of life." – Ravi Zacharias

Themes: Resurrection, Easter, Life, Jesus, Death, Mother-in-law, Holy Land, Israel, Pilgrims, Pilgrimage, Funeral, Funeral Director, Death.

20. CHRISTMAS GIFT

Two brothers, Joe aged 3 and Brandon aged 5 were spending a few days just before Christmas with grandma.

When it was bedtime, Joe was praying at the top of his voice, "O God, please send Santa with a bike for Christmas."

Brandon: "Why are you shouting? God is not deaf."

Joe: "Yes, I know God is not deaf, but grandma is!"

* * *

The greatest gift of God to humanity is the gift of his only son Jesus Christ. God clearly manifested his immense love for humankind by sending the Messiah.

The best Christmas gift you can give to others is the gift of the Savior Jesus Christ. Share the precious gift with your family and friends.

"You give but little when you give of your possessions. It is when you give of yourself that you truly give." – Kahlil Gibran

"The best of all gifts around any Christmas tree: the presence of a happy family all wrapped up in each other." - Burton Hillis

Themes: Christmas, Gifts, Santa clause, God, Jesus Christ, Redeemer, Savior, Evangelization, Grandma.

21. ROOM IN THE INN

Second graders are staging a nativity play around Christmas time. The scene is Joseph and Mary knocking at the door of the innkeeper.

The innkeeper comes out and says, "Can't you see the 'No Vacancy' sign?"

Joseph retorts, "Can't you see that my wife is pregnant and is about to give birth to a baby?"

Innkeeper: "But that's not my fault!"

Joseph: "That's not my fault either!"

* * *

Make room for Jesus in your heart. He is coming and knocking at the door of your heart now. You have to open the door from inside and allow Him in. The handle of the door is on your side. He will not force His way in.

If your life is full of greed, avarice, hatred, anger, envy, pride, immorality, Jesus will have no place. Empty yourself. Make room for Him.

Be willing to make room for what God is preparing for you.

"If one has the answers to all the questions – that is the proof that God is not with him. It means that he is a false prophet using religion for himself. The great leaders of the people of God, like Moses, have always left room for doubt. You must leave room for the Lord, not for our certainties; we must be humble."

– Pope Francis

"Grace is never wanting. God always gives sufficient grace to whoever is willing to receive it." – St. Francis De Sales

Themes: Christmas, Joseph, Mary, Innkeeper, Baby, Fault, Vacancy, Room, Make Room, Materialism, Sins, Humility, Grace.

22. THE HENPECKED HUSBAND

A henpecked husband went to a counselor for assertive training. After the counseling session, he was given a book to read. He read that on his way home.

On entering the house, he called his wife and said, "Today onwards, I am the man of the house. What I say is the law here. You are going to cook a gourmet meal for me. Then you are going to prepare the bathtub for me. Guess, who is going to comb my hair after the bath?"

The wife replied, "The undertaker!"

* * *

Be assertive; do not allow others to control your life. You are responsible for your life and so live your life to the full. Believe in yourself. Say to yourself often: "I can do it."

An assertive person feels free to express his or her feelings, thoughts, and desires. Assertiveness is an attitude: that of defending your rights without hurting those of others.

Self-confidence will enable you to accomplish much in life. It is only if you can see that in yourself will others see it. It's not who you are that holds you back, it's who you think you're not.

"Our ultimate freedom is the right and power to decide how anybody or anything outside ourselves will affect us." – Stephen Covey

"I am not what has happened to me. I am what I choose to become." – Carl Jung

Themes: Assertiveness, Confidence, Self-confidence, Counselor, Husband, Wife, Family, Man, Woman, Undertaker, Life, Death.

23. MISTAKEN IDENTITY

According to a story, Pope Francis arrived in New York for a visit. As he came out of the airport, he told the limousine driver: "Hello, back in Rome, I am not allowed to drive. So can I drive here a little?"

The limo driver said, "Your Holiness, I don't think that's a good idea."

But the pope insisted and the limo driver finally yielded. So the pope got into the driver's seat and the driver went to the passenger seat behind. As they entered the freeway the pope began to press down the pedal racing to a speed of 120 miles per hour. The driver from behind pleaded, "Your Holiness, please don't go that fast; it's too dangerous." Soon the pope reached a speed of about 140 miles per hour.

Momentarily he was pulled over by a highway patrol officer. The officer went and had a look at the driver's seat and got a shock. So he went and radioed his boss, "Sir, there's a big problem here. I caught a man driving at a speed of 140 miles!"

"Give him a ticket," said the boss.

"No we can't do that; there is a very important person in the limo!"

"Who is he, the mayor of New York?"

"No, someone more important!"

"Is it the governor?"

"No, someone more important!"

"Is he the president?"

"No, someone more important!"

"Tell me, who the hell is he?"

"I think it is God himself, because he has the Pope as the driver!"

* * *

Who or what is driving your life? Everyone's life is driven by somebody or something. Have vision and mission in life and that could be your driving force in life. Live a purpose-driven life.

Believe in yourself and believe you can, and you are half-way there. The first step or the beginning is the hardest. If you start now you'll start seeing results one day earlier than if you wait until tomorrow. Start today. Be better than you were yesterday.

"Desire is the key to motivation, but it's determination and commitment to an unrelenting pursuit of your goal – a commitment to excellence – that will enable you to attain the success you seek." – Mario Andretti

"The two most important days in your life are the day you are born, and the day you find out why." – Mark Twain

Themes: Drive, Motivation, Purpose, Identity, Pope, Driver, Ambition, Desire, Direction.

24. iPad for Christmas

Dear Jesus,
If you ever want to see your mother agian...

It was Christmas time; the four-year old Tim asked his mom if he could get an iPad as Christmas gift. The mother told him to write a letter to Baby Jesus.

So he took a sheet of paper and wrote: "Dear Jesus, I have been a good boy always, please send me an iPad for Christmas." Then he read it and said to himself, "That is not true."

He tore that up and took another sheet and wrote: "Dear Jesus, I have been a good boy sometimes, please send me an iPad for Christmas." But he knew that too is not true.

He ripped that sheet of paper too and wrote again on another, "Dear Jesus, I will be a good boy." When he read that, he did not feel comfortable. So he tore up that paper, too.

Then he went for a walk in the neighborhood. He came to a church where there was the nativity scene displayed. He took the statue of mother Mary and hid it inside his overcoat and returned home. He went up straight to his room and hid the statue under the bed. Then he took a sheet of paper and wrote, "Dear Jesus, if you want to see your mother again … "

* * *

Prayer is communication with God. This communication will become easier, if you have a personal relationship with God. When you are in love with Him, you will want to be in His presence often and converse with Him.

Have great faith when you pray. Believe that God is going to give you what you ask of Him. Have an attitude of gratitude. When you are deeply grateful, you will be abundantly blessed.

"Prayer is the key of the morning and the bolt of the evening." – Mahatma Gandhi

"A grateful heart is a beginning of greatness. It is an expression of humility. It is a foundation for the development of such virtues as prayer, faith, courage, contentment, happiness, love, and well-being." – James E. Faust

Themes: Prayer, Faith, Gratitude, Thanksgiving, Christmas, Gift, iPad, Jesus, Mom, Mother, Mary, Goodness, Naughty, Church, Nativity, Threat, Ransom.

25. Flight Training

A baby mosquito was given flying lessons by the mother mosquito. Once the baby mosquito graduated from the school of the mother, it was allowed to take off alone.

After the first day of hunting alone, the baby mosquito returned to the mother. The anxious mom asked, "How was your day?"

The baby mosquito replied, "These human beings are so very nice! Wherever I went they were clapping for me!"

* * *

Be generous with your appreciation of others. Make people around you feel good and important. You bring out the best in others through sincere appreciation. Remember to celebrate others. Recall their birthdays and anniversaries.

Do not wait till their death to say good things about them. Offer affection and gratitude when they are alive. Life is too short and so show your appreciation for others today.

No duty is more important than returning thanks. When you

show gratitude to others, they will want to do more favors for you.

"Appreciation is a wonderful thing: It makes what is excellent in others belong to us as well." – Voltaire

"Appreciation can make a day, even change a life. Your willingness to put it into words is all that is necessary." – Margaret Cousins

Themes: Appreciation, Praise, Applause, Gratitude, Thanksgiving, Thankfulness, Positive strokes.

26. FAITH FROM THE SOURCE

A Jewish man was becoming increasingly nervous. His son was coming of age and his 13th year was drawing closer. The man was concerned that his young son was not well versed in the Jewish faith and wanted to better educate him on his roots before his bar Mitzvah. The father decided to send his young son to Israel to see their homeland and study his heritage.

The time came for the young boy to return home. The boy came in and fell to his father's feet thanking him over and over for sending him to Israel. "Oh father" he exclaimed excitedly. "I learned so much while I was there ... but I have some bad news" pausing a second or so he concluded: "While I was there I converted to Christianity."

The father fell to his knees "Oh, no! What have I done?"

Worried he rushed to his closest friend's house. After explaining what happened to him, his friend replied: "Funny you should bring this to me! I also sent my son to Israel and he too converted to Christianity!"

The two friends in their distress decided they must immediately go to the Rabbi and ask for guidance. After explaining the Rabbi replied: "Funny you should bring this to me. I too sent my son to Israel and he also converted to Christianity!"

All three men in unison fell to their knees and blurted out prayers to God begging for guidance. God quietly replied: "Funny you should bring this to me ... I, too, sent my son to Israel!"

***

The Christmas mystery offers to us and to the whole world a fundamental truth about God, that God is not distant.

God is Emanuel. God is with us. The Infant Jesus of Bethlehem who is truly God is also truly one of us. God is enfleshed in the Infant Jesus and is born of the Virgin Mary.

At Christmas, we celebrate God's great act of love. We recall the story of God becoming human in the person of Jesus Christ. Every celebration of Jesus' birthday should draw us closer to Him and help us grow in our personal relationship with Him.

"Christmas, my child, is love in action." – Dale Evans Rogers

"This is the message of Christmas: we are never alone." – Taylor Caldwell

Themes: God, Christmas, Emanuel, Incarnation, Love, Conversion, Christian, Rabbi, Israel, Christianity, Son, Father, Jewish, Faith.

27. PALM SUNDAY

A little boy was sick on Palm Sunday and stayed home from church with his mother. His father returned from church holding a palm branch. The little boy was curious and asked, *"Why do you have that palm branch, dad?"*

"You see, when Jesus came into town, everyone waved palm branches to honor him, so we got palm branches today. " The little boy replied, "Too bad! The one Sunday I miss, Jesus shows up!"

***

Sunday is a day to refuel your soul and be grateful for God's blessings. There is no greater act of worship than giving yourself totally to God. A Sunday well spent brings a week of contentment.

When you gather for the Sunday, recognize the presence of the Triune God in the assembly gathered for worship, in the minister officiating, in the Word of God that is proclaimed and above all in the bread and wine transformed into the Body and Blood of Christ.

God is present everywhere: in you, in others, in the universe. The practice of the presence of God will lead you to consciousness. Some people complain they don't feel God's presence in their lives. The truth is, God manifests Himself to us everyday; we just fail to recognize him.

"Where can I hide from your spirit? From your presence, where can I flee? If I ascend to the heavens, you are there; if I lie down in Sheol, you are there too." – Psalms 139:7-8

"We cannot spend our entire week in pursuit of the world and then wonder why our worship on Sunday feels flat." – Joel Balin

Themes: Palm Sunday, Jesus, Church, Obligation, Sunday, Recognition, Presence of God, Boy, Mother, Father.

28. HEAVENLY DELIGHT

A cat died and went to Heaven. St Peter met her at the gates and said, "You have been a good cat all these years. Anything you want is yours for the asking."

The cat thought for a minute and then said, "All my life I lived on a farm and slept on hard wooden floors. I would like a real fluffy pillow to sleep on."

St Peter said, "Say no more." Instantly the cat had a huge fluffy pillow.

A few days later, six mice were killed in an accident and they all went to heaven together. St Peter met the mice at the gates with the same offer that He made to the cat.

The mice said, "Well, we have had to run all of our lives: from cats, dogs, and even people with brooms! If we could just have some little roller skates, we would not have to run again."

St Peter answered, "It is done." All the mice had beautiful little roller skates.

About a week later, St Peter decided to check on the cat. He found her sound asleep on her fluffy pillow. He gently awakened the cat and asked, "Is everything okay? How have you been doing? Are you happy?"

The cat replied, "Oh, it is wonderful! I have never been so happy in my life. The pillow is so fluffy, and those little Meals on Wheels you have been sending over are delicious!"

* * *

See beauty and abundance all around you. Happiness, joy and contentment are an inside job. The provider is the same for all. Always be content with what you have, because God knows what's best for you.

Satisfaction in life arises from knowing you are exactly where you belong. Discontented people strive to be somewhere else or someone else. Contentment comes from accepting great and small things that come your way.

Stop looking for reasons to be unhappy. Focus on the things you do have, and the reasons you should be happy.

"It is not what we take up, but what we give up, that makes us rich." – Henry Ward Beecher

"Two men looked out from prison bars, one saw the mud, the other saw the stars." – Frederick Langbridge

Themes: God, Heaven, Cat, Mice, Happiness, Joy, Meals, Contentment, Satisfaction, Vision, Visualization.

29. HEALING TOUCH

Three men were fishing in the Sea of Galilee one day, when Jesus walked across the water and joined them in the boat. When the three astonished men had settled down and calmed themselves to be able to speak, the first man asked humbly, "Jesus, I've suffered from back pain ever since I lifted heavy shrapnel in the Vietnam War. Could you help me?" "Of course, my son," Jesus said and touched the man's back. The man felt relief for the first time in years.

The second man, who wore very thick glasses and had a hard time reading and driving, asked if Jesus could do anything about his poor eyesight. Jesus smiled, removed the man's glasses and tossed them into the lake. When they hit the water, the man's eyes cleared and he could see everything distinctly.

When Jesus turned to the third man, the man put his hands out defensively. "Don't touch me!" he cried. "I'm on a disability pension!"

* * *

The key to success is hard work and determination. It is said that all roads that lead to success have to pass through hard work boulevard at some point. While most are dreaming of success, winners wake-up and work hard to achieve it. No pain, no gain.

Hard work brings about long lasting results because there is focus and intensity. Lack of natural talent is irrelevant to great success. Many ordinary people have become extraordinary, thanks to sheer hard work.

"The three great essentials to achieve anything worthwhile are: hard work, stick-to-itiveness, and common sense." – Thomas A. Edison

"Striving for success without hard work is like trying to harvest where you haven't planted." – David Bly

Themes: Jesus, Men, Hard work, Industrious, Diligence, Success, Conscientious, Lazy, Disability, Pension, Suffering, Healing, Health, Sea of Galilee.

30. FAR SIGHT

Two blondes living in Oklahoma were sitting on a bench talking ... and one blonde says to the other:

"Which do you think is farther away - Florida or the moon?"

The other blonde turns and says: "Hello can you see Florida?

* * *

A good vision identifies direction and purpose for any organization. It sets standards of excellence that reflect high ideals and a sense of integrity. It is well articulated and easily understood. It challenges and inspires people to align their energies in a common direction. It brings about efficiency and productivity.

We are limited not by our abilities but by our vision. There is a Japanese proverb that says: "Vision without action is daydream. Action without vision is nightmare."

"The most pathetic person in the world is someone who has sight, but has no vision." – Helen Keller

"In order to carry a positive action we must develop here a positive vision." – Dalai Lama

"The eye through which I see God is the same eye through which God sees me; my eye and God's eye are one eye, one seeing, one knowing, one love." – Meister Eckhart

Themes: Vision, Foresight, Sight, Blonde, Planning, Goals, Action,

31. RESOURCEFUL NUN

A young nun who worked for a local home health care agency was out making her rounds when she ran out of gas. As luck would have it there was a gas station just one block away. She walked to the station to borrow a can with enough gas to start the car and drive to the station for a fill up.

The attendant regretfully told her that the only gas can he owned had just been loaned out, but if she would care to wait he was sure it would be back shortly. Since the nun was on the way to see a patient, she decided not to wait and walked back to her car.

After looking through her car for something to carry to the station to fill with gas, she spotted a bedpan she was taking to the patient. Always resourceful, she carried it to the station, filled it with gasoline, and carried it back to her car. As she was pouring the gas into the tank of her car two men watched her from across the street.

One of them turned to the other and said: "I know that it is said that Jesus turned water into wine, but if that car starts, I'll become a Catholic for the rest of my life!"

* * *

Being resourceful means being proactive. The people who get things done are resourceful. Life doesn't hand out ready solutions to address the problems and situations we encounter.

A resourceful person is someone who can figure things out by oneself in a difficult situation. Resourceful persons are capable of figuring out solutions to problems using creative methods. They use available resources to help solve problems or overcome obstacles.

The first step towards getting somewhere is deciding that you are not going to stay where you are.

"It is not resources but resourcefulness that ultimately makes the difference." – Tony Robbins

"A resourceful person can see opportunity when others only see obstacles." – Garrett Gunderson

Themes: Resourcefulness, Ingenuity, Invention, Creativity, Originality, Faith, Nun, Sisters, Religious, Gas, Bedpan, Men, Catholic.

32. GET YOUR ACT TOGETHER

A police officer stops a blonde for speeding and asks her very nicely if he could see her license.

She replied in a huff, "I wish you guys would get your act together. Just yesterday you take away my license and then today you expect me to show it to you!"

* * *

A good organization is expected to get its act together. No business can succeed without having a proper organizational structure. That calls for drawing up plans, setting goals, and working harmoniously. All should be on the same page. Effective communication is vital.

A beehive is an example of division of labor and unity of purpose. In a good music show, the instrumentation, harmony, counterpoint are to be well coordinated to create a great effect. A charismatic leader with passion can bring about teamwork and cooperation. You have to openly share information, knowledge and expertise with the team and co-workers.

The success of any organization primarily depends upon how good the management of the organization is.

"The achievements of an organization are the results of the combined effort of each individual." – Vince Lombardi

"Not everything that is faced can be changed, but nothing can be changed until it is faced." – James Baldwin

Themes: Organization, Leaders, Police, Union, Group, Company, Business, Unity, Harmony, Orchestra, Blonde, License, Car, Speeding.

33. LUMBER THIEF

Jack worked in the lumberyard for twenty years and all that time he'd been stealing the wood and selling it.

At last his conscience began to bother him and he went to confession to repent. Father, it's 15 years since my last confession, and I've been stealing wood from the lumber yard all these years," he told the priest.

"I understand my son," says the priest. "As penance can you make a Novena?"

Jack said, "Yes Father, if you have the plans ready, I've enough lumber."

* * *

People take away things like office supplies consciously or unconsciously for personal use. When they do that, they are showing that they lack those things or do not have the ability to buy them themselves. When you operate from a lack mentality, you will always lack those things.

Sincerity will give you peace of mind and enable you to be confident. People do appreciate authentic persons. If you are your authentic self, you have no competition.

"To practice five things under all circumstances constitutes perfect virtue; these five are gravity, generosity of soul, sincerity, earnestness, and kindness."

– Confucius

"The mind is a terrible thing to waste. Think positive thoughts. Don't allow negative influences to steal your joy. Remember,

43

life is 10 percent what happens to you and 90 percent how you respond." – Joel Osteen

Themes; Stealing, Theft, Robbery, Honesty, Sincerity, Generosity, Earnestness, Kindness, Thief, Confession, Conscience, Novena.

34. BASEBALL FANS

Two friends were extremely interested in baseball. So they wished and hoped that there would be baseball in heaven. Not being certain, they agreed that whomever dies first would come back and report to the other.

After a few years, one of them died. The one who died, came back and told the other: "There is good news and bad news. The good news is that there is baseball in heaven. The bad news is that you are scheduled to pitch next Thursday!"

* * *

No human being has lived forever. Since we do not know when death will come, we have to be prepared always. The Bible says, "You also must be prepared, for at an hour you do not expect, the Son of Man will come." (Matthew 24:44) There are people who buy a casket and place it in a prominent place in the house to remind themselves of death. There are still others who get caskets ahead of time and lie down in it for a few minutes everyday as if to practice for death. You don't have to be so crazy.

What is important is to put life in order. Be at peace and be reconciled with God and one another. Prepare your will and testament. If you make your funeral plans and arrangements ahead of time, it will be much easier for your dear ones when you die.

"Somebody should tell us, right at the start of our lives, that we are dying. Then we might live life to the limit, every minute of every day. Do it!, I say. Whatever you want to do, do it now! There are only so many tomorrows." – Pope Paul VI

"There is only so much you can do in anticipation of a loss, but you can prepare yourself by trying to review your relationships and tie up loose ends." – Gerald Shiener

Themes: Death, Life, Preparation, Funeral, Will and Testament, Heaven, Eternity, Friends, Baseball.

35. FORGIVE US OUR TRESPASSES

In a large city, a priest parked his car in a no-parking zone because he couldn't find a metered space. He put a note under the windshield wiper that read: "I have circled the block 10 times. If I don't park here, I'll miss my appointment. "FORGIVE US OUR TRESPASSES."

When he returned, he found a citation from a police officer along with this note: "I've circled this block for 10 years. If I don't give you a ticket, I'll lose my job. "LEAD US NOT INTO TEMPTATION."

* * *

God does forgive our trespasses. He is merciful and loving even to the worst offenders. He is a fountain of mercy and grace. No matter what you have done, when you repent, God pardons. God loves you no matter how great your sins are. He wants you to recognize that His mercy is greater than your sins.

God wants you to approach Him in prayer and beg Him to pour His mercy out upon you and the whole world. God wants you to receive His mercy and let it flow through you to others. God wants you to know that graces of His mercy are dependent upon your trust.

"Look into my heart and see there the love and mercy which I have for humankind, and especially for sinners. Look, and enter into my passion." – Jesus to St. Faustina (Diary 1663)

"Those who sincerely say 'Jesus, I trust in you' will find comfort in all their anxieties and fear." – St. Pope John Paul II

Themes: Temptations, Mercy, Divine Mercy, Forgiveness, Priest, Trespasses, Cop, Police Officer, Citation.

36. YOUR NAME PLEASE

One weekend my friend Sally, a nurse, was looking after her six-year-old nephew when he fell off a playground slide and hit his head.

Worried that he might have a concussion, she checked him all night.

Every hour, she'd gently shake him and ask, "What's your name?" Soon, he began moaning in protest each time she entered the room.

When Sally went in at 5:00 A.M., she found something white on his forehead. Leaning close, she saw a crayon-scrawled message taped to his forehead.

It read: "My name is Daniel."

* * *

Know who you are. Knowing yourself means respecting your core values, principles, beliefs, personality, relationships and your beautiful body. Know your strengths and weaknesses. It also means knowing why you are here on earth.

You have to make conscious efforts to get to know yourself. Ask yourself: "Who am I now?" and "What makes me happy?" God has made you unique and so do not be afraid to be different. Make time for brief moments of solitude to connect with yourself. Meditation can help you to discover yourself.

"It takes courage to grow up and become who you really are." - E.E. Cummings

"The day came when the risk to remain tight in a bud was more painful than the risk it took to blossom." – Anais Nin

Themes: Self Knowledge, Knowing Yourself, Core Values, Happiness, , Name.

37. Crossing the Sea of Galilee

An American, planning a trip to the Holy Land, was aghast when he found it would cost $100 dollars an hour to rent a boat on the Sea of Galilee.

He said, "In America it wouldn't be more than $50."

"That might be true," said the travel agent, "but you have to take into account that the Sea of Galilee is water on which our Lord Himself walked."

"Well, at $100 an hour for a boat," said the American, "it's no wonder He walked."

* * *

Walking is good for your health and fitness. An adult needs 30 minutes of physical activity daily. A regular walk will help to maintain body weight, reduce heart disease, improve blood pressure and enhance mental well being.

If you walk with another person, it will give you time for socializing and developing a relationship. Having a dog helps people to take it for a walk, as the dog needs exercise. If you walk outdoors, you can enjoy the season and the beautiful creation of God.

"Another thing I like to do is sit back and take in nature. To look at the birds, listen to their singing, go hiking, camping and jogging and running, walking along the beach, playing games and sometimes being alone with the great outdoors. It's very special to me." – Larry Wilcox

"Beauty surrounds us, but usually we need to be walking in a garden to know it." – Rumi

Themes: Walking, Hiking, Jogging, Running, Camping, Stroll, Holy Land, American, Sea of Galilee, Boat, Health, Fitness, Relationship.

38. GIVE ME TIME

Two elderly ladies have been friends for many decades. Over the years they had shared all kinds of activities and adventures. Lately, their activities had been limited to meeting a few times a week to play cards.

One day they were playing cards when one looked at the other and said, "Now don't get mad at me ... I know we've been friends for a long time ... but I just can't think of your name! I've thought and thought, but I can't remember it. Please tell me what your name is."

Her friend glared at her. For at least three minutes she just stared at her. Finally she said, "How soon do you need to know?"

* * *

Good friends will bring the best out of you. They make your lives interesting and wonderful. He or she will be there for you not only at joyous occasions but also at painful moments of life. A good friend will stand by you when the whole world is against you.

Your friends do influence and improve your life. If your best friend eats healthy food, you are more likely to have healthy diet yourself. You can learn important skills from them.

"In poverty and other misfortunes of life, true friends are a sure refuge. They keep the young out of mischief; they comfort and aid the old in their weakness, and they incite those in the prime of life to noble deeds." – Aristotle

"Don't walk behind me; I may not lead. Don't walk in front

of me; I may not follow. Just walk beside me and be my friend."
– Albert Camus

Themes: Friendship, Friend, Relationship, Companionship, Elderly, Influence, Time.

39. LENTEN DISCIPLINE

John Smith was the only Protestant to move into a large Catholic neighborhood. On the first Friday of Lent, John was outside grilling a big juicy steak on his grill. Meanwhile, all of his neighbors were eating cold tuna fish for supper. This went on each Friday of Lent.

On the last Friday of Lent, the neighborhood men got together and decided that something had to be done about John, he was tempting them to eat meat each Friday of Lent, and they couldn't take it anymore. They decided to try and convert John to be a Catholic. They went over and talked to him and were so happy that he decided to join all of his neighbors and become a Catholic.

They took him to church, and the Priest sprinkled some water over him, and said, "You were born a Baptist, you were raised a Baptist, and now you are a Catholic." The men were so relieved, now their biggest Lenten temptation was resolved.

The next year's Lenten season rolled around. The first Friday of Lent came and just at supper time, when the neighborhood was settling down to their tuna fish dinner, came the wafting smell of steak cooking on a grill. The neighborhood men could not believe their noses! What's going on? They called each other up and decided to meet over in John's yard to see if he had forgotten it was the first Friday of Lent?

The group arrived just in time to see John standing over his grill with a small pitcher of water. He was sprinkling some water over his steak on the grill, saying, "You were born a cow, you were raised a cow, and now you are a fish."

* * *

God wants your conversion of heart. A life of turning to God from sin is the mark of true conversion. Turn away from sins and put on Christ. True repentance calls for sincere regret and sorrow for offending God by sins, and a firm resolve not to offend Him again. That is to say, one will not return to former ways of life.

"Being a Christian is more than just an instantaneous conversion – it is a daily process whereby you grow to be more and more like Christ." – Billy Graham

"Conversion to Christ is not merely accepting a set of facts and declaring them to be true. It's assuming a posture of repentance and faith toward the finished work of Christ." – J.D. Greear

Themes: Lent, Conversion, Fasting, Abstinence, Protestant, Baptist, Cow, Fish, God, Christian, Christ.

40. DELIVERY IN DARKNESS

Due to a power outage at the time, only one paramedic responded to the call. The house was very, very dark, so the paramedic asked Katelyn, a 3-year-old girl, to hold a flashlight high over her mom so he could see while he helped deliver the baby. Very diligently, Katelyn did as she was asked.

Heidi pushed and pushed, and after a little while Connor was born. The paramedic lifted him by his little feet and spanked him on his bottom. Connor began to cry.

The paramedic then thanked Katelyn for her help and asked the wide-eyed 3-year old what she thought about what she had just witnessed. Katelyn quickly responded, "He shouldn't have crawled in there in the first place. Smack him again."

* * *

Experts say that rewards are more effective than punishment. When children are rewarded for good behavior, you will get more good behavior from them. Bad behavior cannot be ignored and that has to be dealt with promptly.

In some cases, punishments are effective but not always. Punishment is effective if it is immediately following bad behavior and when applied consistently. It is not effective when any behavior changes that result from punishment are often temporary. Sometimes punishments can also cause unintended and undesirable results.

"Power is of two kinds. One is obtained by the fear of punishment and the other by acts of love. Power based on love is a thousand times more effective and permanent than the one derived from fear of punishment." – Mahatma Gandhi

"To work without attachment is to work without the expectation of reward or fear of any punishment in this world or the next. Work so done is a means to the end, and God is the end." – Ramakrishna

Themes: Punishment, Penalty, Price, Reward, Behavior, Love, God.

41. DIRECTION TO THE POST OFFICE

The Reverend Billy Graham tells of a time early in his career when he arrived in a small town to preach a sermon. Wanting to mail a letter, he asked a young boy directions to the post office.

After being told the way by the lad, the Reverend Graham thanked him, adding: "If you'll come to the Baptist church this evening, you can hear me telling everyone how to get to Heaven.

"I don't think I'll be there," the boy said. "You don't even know your way to the post office."

* * *

When you are new to a place, you can be easily lost. But today there are GPS and maps to guide you. Suppose you asked a person for direction and he explained to you the route pretty well, you will be happy. But you will be happier, if he says that he will go with you to show that place.

Jesus said, "I am the way and the truth and the life. No one comes to the Father except through me." (John 14:6). Jesus has shown you the way. He has traced out the way to heaven in the pages of the Scriptures. If you follow the direction that He has given you, you will never be lost.

"I can't change the direction of the wind, but I can adjust my sails to always reach my destination." – Jimmy Dean

"The fragrance of flowers spreads only in the direction the wind. But the goodness of a person spreads in all directions." – Chanakya

Themes: Way, Direction, Plan, Goal, Vision, Billy Graham, Baptist Church, Heaven, Post Office.

42. IMPORTANCE OF GOOD BEHAVIOR

It was the first day of school. The previous principal had just retired and a new principal just started. As the principal made his rounds, he heard a terrible commotion coming from one of the classrooms. He rushed in and spotted one boy, taller than the others, who seemed to be making the most noise. He seized the lad, dragged him to the hall, gave him his sternest look, and told him to wait there until he was excused.

Returning to the classroom, the principal restored order and lectured the class for half an hour about the importance of good behavior.

When he finished he said, "Now, are there any questions about anything I just said?"

One girl stood up very timidly. "Sir, is our teacher going to be out in the hall very long?"

* * *

Some kids are good and they never get into trouble. They never cause problems for the parents and teachers. In contrast there are children who are rude and troublesome.

Parents need to teach children to manage their emotions in a mature way. Teach them social skills to get along well with others.

Children do as you do because you are the role model for them. Tell them sincerely how their behavior affects you. Be more positive than negative towards your kids. Help them build good habits and make them stick.

"The most powerful leadership tool you have is your own personal example." – John Wooden

"People may hear your words, but they feel your attitude." John C. Maxwell

Themes: School, Principal, Discipline, Behavior, Personal Example, Words, Attitude, Kids, Children, Parents, Emotions, Skills, Social Skills, Role Model, Habits.

43. IT'S A HORSE

When a husband was quietly reading his newspaper, his wife came from behind and hit on his head with a frying pan. "What was that for?" he asked.

His wife replied: "That was for a piece of paper that I found with the name Mary Lou on it in your pocket."

"Oh that is the name of the horse that I was betting last night on the race track," said the husband. She apologized and went on her business.

Two days later, the wife hit his head again with a bigger frying pan. "What in the world was that for?" he asked.

She replied: "Your horse just called."

* * *

Being faithful to your spouse will help you stay in the relationship. When people are deeply committed to their spouses and marriage, they make sacrifices for the sake of their marriage and enjoy long-lasting marriages.

Wear your wedding ring always and that will remind you of your vows. Trust your partner that he or she will not cheat on you. Keep your marriage a priority and put it before everything else.

"Marriage has a unique place because it speaks of an absolute faithfulness, a covenant between radically different persons, male and female; and so it echoes the absolute covenant of God with his chosen, a covenant between radically different partners." – Rowan D. Williams

"Health is the greatest gift, contentment the greatest wealth, faithfulness the best relationship." – Buddha

Themes: Faithfulness, Marriage, God, Covenant, Partners, Relationship, Horse, Betting, Wife, Husband, Cheating.

44. APPROPRIATE HYMNS

There was a feud between the Pastor and the Choir Director of a Baptist church. It seems the first hint of trouble came when the Pastor preached on "Dedicating oneself to service" and the Choir Director chose to sing: *"I Shall Not Be Moved."*

Trying to believe it was a coincidence, the Pastor put the incident behind him. The next Sunday he preached on "giving". Afterwards, the choir squirmed as the director led them in the hymn: *"Jesus Paid It All."* By this time, the Pastor was losing his temper. Sunday morning attendance swelled as the tension between the two built.

A large crowd showed up the next week to hear his sermon on the "sin of gossiping." Would you believe the Choir Director selected, *"I Love to Tell the Story."* There was no turning back.

The following Sunday the Pastor told the congregation that unless something changed he was considering resignation. The entire church gasped when the Choir Director led them in: *"Why Not Tonight?"*

Truthfully, no one was surprised when the Pastor resigned a week later, explaining that Jesus had led him there and Jesus was leading him away. The Choir Director could not resist singing, *"What A Friend We Have In Jesus."*

* * *

Because of your differences, when people come together, there is often conflict. Resolve internal conflicts effectively for the success of any organization, church or business. It can be detrimental to the morale of the workplace and results you achieve.

Conflict resolution is often achieved by addressing it through negotiation, mediation, diplomacy, and creative peace building.

"Blessed are the peacemakers, for they will be called children of God." Matthew 5:9

"Forgiveness is the fragrance that the violet sheds on the heel that has crushed it." – Mark Twain

"The weak can never forgive. Forgiveness is the attribute of the strong." – Mahatma Gandhi

Themes: Jesus, Feud, Strife, Dispute, Conflict, Peace, Reconciliation, Forgiveness, Giving, Sin, Gossip, Change, Resignation, Hymns, Pastor, Musician, Cantor, Choir, Director, Baptist, Church.

45. HAVING SIMILAR WEDDING

Little Tommy was so impressed by his oldest sister's wedding that he announced: "I want to have a wedding just like Linda had."

"That sounds great," said his father. "But whom will you marry?"

Tommy announced: "I want to marry grandma because she loves me and I love her."

"You can't marry grandma," his father said.

"Why not?" Tommy protested. "Because she is my mother."

"Well," reasoned Tommy. "Then why did you marry my mother?"

* * *

Marriage is sacred and so you should not enter into it lightly. It is a holy relationship between two people and you have to work hard to sustain it.

A great marriage is not when the perfect couple come together. It is when an imperfect couple learns to enjoy their differences.

Good communication, sacrificial love, forgiveness and praying together can contribute a great deal towards a happy marriage.

Marriage is when two people become one, but the problem starts when they try to decide which one.

"A successful marriage requires falling in love many times, always with the same person." – Mignon McLaughlin

"Marriage is three parts love and seven parts forgiveness of sins." – Lao Tzu

Themes: Marriage, Wedding, Matrimony, Love, Relationship, Ritual, Forgiveness, Father, Grandmother, Boy, Sister, Father, Grandma.

46. ROLE CHANGE

A man who had been a husband for ten years was consulting a marriage counselor. "When I was first married I was very happy. When I came home from a hard day at the shop, my little dog would race around barking and my wife would bring me my slippers with a heartwarming smile. Now after all these years everything is changed. Now when I come home, my dog brings me my slippers and my wife barks at me."

"I don't know what you are complaining about," said the counselor. "You are still getting the same service."

* * *

If a marriage has to last forever, there has to be unconditional sacrificial love between the spouses. Ask yourself daily: "How can I serve my spouse better?" Christ's love for you is unconditional, and that is the love you are to seek in marriage.

Love is about sacrifice. When you love someone, you want to sacrifice your time, talent and treasure for the sake of that person.

When a man opens the car door for his wife, one thing is sure, either the car is new or the wife is new.

When nails grow long, we cut nails not fingers. Similarly, when misunderstandings grow up, cut your ego, not your relationship.

"Love is patient, love is kind. It is not jealous, love is not pompous, it is not inflated, it is not rude, it does not seek its own interests, it is not quick-tempered, it does not brood over injury, it does not rejoice over wrongdoing but rejoices with the truth. It bears all things, believes all things, hopes all things, endures all things." – 1 Corinthians 13:4-7

"The best thing to hold onto in life is each other." Audrey Hepburn

Theme: Marriage, Wedding, Matrimony, Ritual, Relationship, Service, Love, Home, Dog, Husband, Wife, Counselor, Counseling.

47. PLANNED MARRIED LIFE

Two senior ladies met for the first time since graduating from high school. One asked the other, "You were always so organized in school, meticulously planning every detail. How did you plan your married life?"

"Well," said her friend, "My first marriage was to a millionaire; my second marriage was to an actor; my third marriage was to a preacher; and now I'm married to an undertaker."

Asked the friend, "What do those marriages have to do with a well-planned life?"

"The first marriage was for the money, the second for the show, the third to get ready and the fourth to go!"

* * *

Good planning gives you peace of mind. Planning will help you to work out what you want to do and achieve what you want. Making a plan will help you to think about how you are going to achieve what you want and work out any extra supports you might need. Having a plan B is very useful. A plan is only as good as those who see it through. Before you start anything, learn how to finish it.

You need short-term and long-term plans. Future depends on long-term planning. People plan for the future based on their current status.

You create your big picture of what you want to do with your life and identify the large-scale goals that you want to achieve. Then, break down into smaller and smaller targets that you must carry out.

"Without goals and plans to reach them, you are like a ship that has set sail with no destination." – Fitzhugh Dodson

"Failing to plan is planning to fail." – Alan Lakein

Themes: Planning, Forethought, Goals, Organization, Preparation, Arrangement, Preacher, Under Taker, Marriage, Millionaire, Actor, Money, Death.

48. PLAYING CHURCH

Johnny's Mother looked out of the window and noticed him "playing church" with their cat. He had the cat sitting quietly and he was preaching to it. She smiled and went about her work.

A while later she heard loud meowing and hissing and ran back to the open window to see Johnny baptizing the cat in a tub of water.

She called out, "Johnny, stop that! The cat is afraid of water!"

Johnny looked up at her and said, "He should have thought about that before he joined my church."

* * *

Baptism is an outward expression of an inward faith. You are sealed by the Holy Spirit in baptism and marked as Christ's own forever.

Why are people baptized? For some it is the decision of the parents because they are infants or children. And they live in that state for the rest of their lives.

Some others enter into baptism just to please someone close to them. It is never a conscious decision or a commitment. Aren't they "playing church?"

What the world needs is not more Christianity but more Christians who practice Christianity. Some Christians are like the candles that have been lit once and then put away in a cupboard to be eaten up by mice.

"The first step on the path to eternal life is baptism." – Delbert L. Stapley

"I believe in Christianity as I believe that the sun has risen: not only because I see it, but because by it I see everything else." – C. S. Lewis

Themes: Foresight, Fear, Baptism, Christening, Faith, Holy Spirit, Parents, Church, Commitment, Eternal Life.

49. THREE TIMES TO CHURCH

Too many people go to Church three times primarily. When they are hatched, matched and dispatched. That is when they're baptized, they get married, and they have their funeral service at the Church. The first time they throw water on you, the second time food, and the third time dirt!

* * *

An action done regularly makes it easier than done occasionally. Consistency is a key to a successful behavior because it leads to habit formation. What you do everyday matters more than what you do once in a while. It can bring about momentum and credibility.

The person who works every single day toward the attainment of his goal will triumph over those who do it once in a while.

Relationship with God is the most important relationship you can have. Trust Him and everything will turn out fine. Even when everyone else only sees our faults, God still sees our possibilities.

"It's not what we do once in a while that shapes our lives. It's what we do consistently." – Tony Robbins

"Consistent action creates consistent results." – Christine Kane

Themes: Consistency, Regularity, Steadiness, Frequency, Mass, Christmas, Easter, Baptism, Marriage, Wedding, Funeral, Action.

50. FINDING JESUS

"Have you found Jesus?" A drunk stumbles across a Pentecostal baptismal service on Sunday afternoon down by the river. He proceeds to walk down into the water and stand next to the Preacher.

The minister turns and notices the old drunk and says, "Mister, are you ready to find Jesus?" The drunk looks back and says, "Yes, Preacher. I sure am."

The minister then dunks the fellow under the water and pulls him right back up. "Have you found Jesus?" the preacher asked. "No, I didn't!" said the drunk.

The preacher then dunks him under for quite a bit longer, brings him up and says, "Now, brother, have you found Jesus?" "No, I did not, Reverend."

The preacher in disgust holds the man under for at least 30 seconds this time, then brings him out of the water and says in a harsh tone, "My God, have you found Jesus yet?" The old drunk wipes his eyes and says to the preacher... "Are you sure this is where he fell in?"

* * *

Poor or lack of communication causes often misunderstanding and broken relationships. It can cause conflict and frustration. Good communication is possible when there is openness on the part of the communicator and listener. And it is a two way process.

Good communication will lead to cooperation and interpersonal relationships.

You can communicate verbally and non-verbally.

Listen actively. Understand the emotion behind the information. The biggest communication problem is we do not listen to understand. We listen to reply.

"Communication leads to community, that is, to understanding, intimacy and mutual valuing." – Rollo May

"Conversion is a complete surrender to Jesus. It's a willingness to do what he wants you to do." – Billy Sunday

Themes: Baptism, Fall, Conversion, Preacher, Minister, Mis-understanding, Communication, Listening.

51. BAPTISMAL POOL

When our church was renovated, adding a baptismal pool, we were pleased. So was our daughter.

While riding in the car with my daughter and her friend, we went past a pond. My daughter's friend proudly declared, "I was baptized in that pond." My daughter responded with no less pride: "Oh, I was baptized in a Jacuzzi at our church."

* * *

Because of the fall of our first parents, we believe that we are born with original sin. Through the sacrament of Baptism the stain of our original sin is washed away. We are made a new creation.

Through baptism we become official members of the Church. We are incorporated into the body of Christ. We become sharers of divine life.

We need to realize that we have great dignity and power in us because of the divine life that we share.

"Go therefore and make disciples of all nations, baptizing them in the name of the Father and of the Son and of the Holy Spirit, teaching them to observe all that I have commanded you." Matthew 28:19-20

"Holy Baptism is the basis of the whole Christian life, the

gateway to life in the Spirit, and the door which gives access to the other sacraments. Through baptism we are freed from sin and reborn as children of God; we become members of Christ, are incorporated into the Church and made sharers in her mission: 'Baptism is a sacrament of regeneration through water in the word." – Catechism of the Catholic Church

Themes: Baptism, Christening, Sacrament, Original sin, Church, Daughter, Friend, First Parents, Body of Christ, Divine Life.

52. INTEREST TO BECOME PRIEST

A mother goes to her pastor and explains that her son seems very interested in becoming a priest. She would like to know what this would require. So the priest begins to explain: "If he wants to become a diocesan priest, he'll have to study for eight years. If he wants to become a Franciscan, he'll have to study for ten years. If he wants to become a Jesuit, he'll have to study for fourteen years." (*This joke originated back when young men entered seminaries right after high school.*)

The mother listens carefully, and as the priest concludes, her eyes brighten. "Sign him up for that last one, Father -- he's a little slow!"

* * *

Everyone has a call or a vocation in life. You have to choose the way of life that you are most drawn and that gives you joy and fulfillment. Every vocation comes from God and so is noble.

Spending time in prayer also will help you in the discernment process. Ask yourself: "What is God's plan for you?"

"Love is the fundamental and innate vocation of every human being." – Catechism of the Catholic Church.

"To be saints is not a privilege for the few, but a vocation for everyone." – Pope Francis

"The power of the priest is the power of the divine person; for the transubstantiation of the bread requires as much power as creation of the world." – St. John Chrysostom

Themes: Priest, Priesthood, Vocation, Call, Religious Life, Franciscan, Jesuit, Clergy, Ministry, Saints.

53. YOU HAVE TO APPLY

A soap manufacturer and a pastor were walking together down a street in a large city. The soap manufacturer casually said, "The gospel you preach hasn't done much good, has it? Just observe. There is still a lot of wickedness in the world, and a lot of wicked people, too!"

The pastor made no reply until they passed a dirty little child making mud pies in the gutter. Seizing the opportunity, the pastor said, "I see that soap hasn't done much good in the world either; for there is much dirt still here, and many dirty people are still around."

The soap man said, "Oh, well, soap only works when it is applied." And the pastor said, "Exactly! So it is with the gospel."

* * *

It is not enough to listen attentively to life transforming messages, but they have to be applied to real life. Put into practice what you have learned. Life can be transformative, if we apply the many principles that you learn.

Most people want others to practice the gospel and live according to moral principles, and not themselves.

Education becomes meaningful when you are able to live what you have learned.

"My life is my message." – Mahatma Gandhi

"An ounce of practice is worth more than tons of preaching." – Mahatma Gandhi

Themes: Christianity, Application, Practice, Action, Education, Messages, Learning Preaching.

54. A TIRED CHRISTMAS SHOPPER

A woman was in the mall doing her Christmas shopping. She was tired of walking through every aisle of every store to find just the right present. She was stressed out by the mounting debt on her credit card. She was tired of fighting the crowds and standing in line for the registers.

Her hands were full and when the elevator door opened, it was full. "Great!" she muttered and the occupants of the elevator, feeling her pain, graciously tightened ranks to allow a small space for her and her load.

As the doors closed she blurted out, "I think whoever came up with this Christmas junk ought to be found, strung up and shot!" A few others shook their heads or grunted in agreement.

Then, from somewhere in the back of the elevator came a single voice that said, "Don't worry. They already crucified him."

* * *

People often forget the reason for the season of Christmas because they are busy shopping, gift giving, decorating, organizing parties, etc. Jesus came with the message of love, peace and joy. Because of your hectic schedule around the season, you may not have time to relish the peace and joy that "the God among us" brought.

It is good to pause everyday during a busy time asking: "Why am I doing what I am doing?" They say everything happens for a reason. Sometimes it would be nice to know that reason.

Don't lose hope. You never know what tomorrow may bring.

"The best of all gifts around any Christmas tree is the presence of a happy family all wrapped up in each other." – Burton Hillis

"My pain may be the reason for somebody's laugh. But my laugh must never be the reason for somebody's pain." – Charlie Chaplain

Themes: Christmas, Christmas Shopping, Gift, Crucifixion, Invention, Stress, Jesus Christ.

55. THE LAST-MINUTE SHOPPER

Typical of last-minute Christmas shoppers, a mother was running furiously from store to store. Suddenly she became aware that the pudgy little hand of her three-year-old son was no longer clutched in hers.

In panic, she retraced her steps and found him standing with his little nose pressed flat against a frosty window. He was gazing at a manger scene.

Hearing his mother's near hysterical call, he turned and shouted with innocent glee: "Look Mommy! It's Jesus - Baby Jesus in the hay!"

With obvious indifference to his joy and wonder, she impatiently jerked him away saying, "We don't have time for that!"

* * *

Everyone can plan and organize their life as well as their time. You often hear the cliché "I don't have time." But all have the same amount of time.

Good time management will lead you to prioritize things in life. You give more time to what you consider are important to you.

At Christmas your priority is to be with Jesus, bathing in the love of the Savior who dwelt among us. Do everything according to the order of importance and arrange according to priority.

"The key is not to prioritize what's on your schedule, but to schedule your priorities." – Stephen Covey

"Time equals life, therefore, waste your time and waste your life, or master your time and master your life." – Alan Lakein

Themes: Prioritization, Time Management, Organization, Planning, Christmas, Christmas Shopping, Shopper, Jesus Christ, Savior.

56. Usher's Dismay

Usher seats Pastor's mother: An elderly woman walked into the local country church. A friendly usher greeted her at the door and helped her up the flight of steps. "Where would you like to sit? He asked.

"The front row please," she answered. "You really don't want to do that," the usher said. "The pastor is really boring with his long homilies."

"Do you happen to know who I am?" asked the woman. "No," said the usher, "I'm the pastor's mother," she replied indignantly. "Do you know who I am?" the usher asked. "No," she said. "Great!" said the usher.

* * *

The truth comes out unknowingly. Sometimes the truth is difficult to swallow. The only people who are mad at you for speaking the truth are those people who are living a lie. Keep speaking the truth.

You need a lot of courage to say who you are and speak out the truth.

People often like to talk at the back of people. Speak well about them. Never say about people in their absence what you would not say in their presence.

"Telling the truth and making someone cry is better than telling a lie and making someone smile." – Paolo Coelho

"Truth is like a lion. You don't have to defend it. Let it loose. It will defend itself." – St. Augustine

Themes: Truth, Recognition, Knowledge, Homily, Sermon, Pastor, Mother, Usher.

57. CEOs

"How many people attend your church?" one pastor asked another. "Five hundred regular, and about five hundred CEO."

"What's CEO?" the first asked. Came the quick answer: "Christmas and Easter Only. We also call them Poinsettias and Easter Lilies."

* * *

Usually the churches are packed for Christmas and Easter. We get twice the usual Sunday crowd on those two holy days of the year.

Many people do not feel the need for God on a daily basis. They think that they are self-sufficient. But when they are in crisis due to bad medical report, loss of job or financial crunch, some turn to God.

The biblical command is to keep the Sabbath holy. If you are spiritually healthy, you will want to have a personal relationship with God. When you are intimately related to Him, you will want to be in His presence as much as possible.

The Bible says: "Come closer to God and God will come closer to you."

"I knew that if I failed I wouldn't regret that, but I knew the one thing I might regret is not trying." – Jeff Bezos

"Don't find fault, find a remedy; anybody can complain." – Henry Ford

Themes: CEO, Christmas, Easter, Sunday, Sabbath, Relationship with God.

58. Drinks for Sisters

A cowgirl, who is visiting Texas from Arkansas, walks into a bar and orders three mugs of Bud. She sits in the back of the room, drinking a sip out of each one in turn.

When she finishes them, she comes back to the bar and orders three more. The bartender approaches and tells the cowgirl, "You know, a mug goes flat after I draw it. It would taste better if you bought one at a time."

The cowgirl replies, "Well, you see, I have two sisters. One is in Australia, the other is in Dublin. When we all left our home in Arkansas, we promised that we'd drink this way to remember the days when we drank together. So I'm drinking one beer for each of my sisters and one for myself."

The bartender admits that this is a nice custom, and leaves it there. The cowgirl becomes a regular in the bar, and always drinks the same way. She orders three mugs and drinks them in turn.

One day, she comes in and only orders two mugs. All the regulars take notice and fall silent. When she comes back to the bar for the second round, the bartender says, "I don't want to intrude on your grief, but I wanted to offer my condolences on your loss."

The cowgirl looks quite puzzled for a moment, then a light dawns in her eyes and she laughs. "Oh, no, everybody's just fine," she explains, "It's just that my husband and I joined the Baptist Church and I had to quit drinking." "Hasn't affected my sisters though."

* * *

You have to live your life and not someone else's life. Know who you are and live the life you are meant to be.

Work for a cause, not for applause. If it's not sincere and genuine, it will never touch another heart.

Be authentic. When you are authentic your words and actions will match. Others will easily see your genuineness or your duplicity. Authenticity requires a certain measure of vulnerability, transparency, and integrity. Don't trade in your authenticity for approval.

"Happiness is when what you think, what you say, and what you do are in harmony." – Mahatma Gandhi

"Authenticity is the daily practice of letting go of who we

think we're supposed to be and embracing who we are." - Brene Brown

Themes: Genuineness, Authenticity, Duplicity, Drinking, Alcoholism, Pretention, Concern, Sympathy, Habits.

59. BLONDE'S BET

Homer, a handsome dude, walked into a sports bar just before 10:00 pm, and sat down next to a blonde.

Staring up at the TV, he saw the 10:00 news had just come on. The news crew was covering a story of a man on a ledge of a large building preparing to jump.

The blonde looked at Homer and said, "Do you think he'll jump?"

Homer answered, "You know, I bet he'll jump."

The blonde replied, "Well, I bet he won't."

Homer placed $20 on the bar and said, "You're on!"

Just as the blonde placed her money on the bar, the guy did a swan dive off of the building, falling to his death.

The blonde was very upset and handed her $20 to Homer, saying, "Fair's fair. Here's your money."

Homer replied, "I can't take your money, I saw this earlier on the 5 o'clock news and knew he would jump."

The blonde replied, "I saw it too; but I didn't think he'd be stupid enough to do it again."

Homer took the money.

* * *

Most disagreements are caused by different perceptions that created different realities. When you make the same mistakes over and over again, you would be considered stupid. You don't want to fall into the same hole a second time.

Do you learn from your mistakes and the mistakes of others? Experience is the best teacher only if we take advantage of it.

Life is all about perception. Positive versus negative. Whichever you choose will affect and more than likely reflect your outcomes.

"Your reality is as you perceive it to be. So, it is true, that by altering this perception we can alter our reality." – William Constantine.

"Men are disturbed not by the things that happen, but by their opinion of the things that happen." – Epictetus

Themes: Perception, Reality, Habit, Experience, Mistakes, Blond, Positive, Negative.

60. UNDERSTANDING OFFICER

A blond was pulled over for speeding by an officer who happened to be a blond. The officer walked up to the driver and demanded to see the driver's license.

After digging into her purse for a while she asked: "What does it look like?"

"It has your picture on it," replied the cop.

The driver handed a little mirror to the officer who looked at it and said: "You can go. I didn't know that you were an officer like me."

* * *

Who are you? You don't need a driver's license to prove your identity. It is when you live your life that you reveal your true identity. Discover the reason for being. Live a purpose-driven life.

Live the life you are meant to live and not what your parents, teachers, pastors, community etc. have told you. Discover who you are and live your life. Then you will be filled with an abundance of joy and fulfillment.

"Most people are other people. Their thoughts are someone else's opinions, their lives a mimicry, their passions a quotation." – Oscar Wilde

"In life you'll realize that there is a purpose for every person you meet. Some are there to test you, some will use you, some will teach you and some will bring out the best in you." – Unknown

Themes: Identity, Purpose of life, Police Officer, Blond, Picture, Photo.

61. RELIGIOUS LEADERS' FLIGHT

A minister, a priest and a rabbi went for a hike one very hot day. They were sweating profusely by the time they came upon a small lake with a sandy beach. Since it was a secluded spot, they left all their clothes on a big log, ran down the beach to the lake and jumped in the water for a long, refreshing swim.

Refreshed, they were halfway back up the beach to the spot they'd left their clothes, when a group of ladies from town came along. Unable to get to their clothes in time, the minister and the priest covered their privates and the rabbi covered his face while they ran for cover in the bushes.

After the ladies wandered on and the men got dressed again, the minister and the priest asked the rabbi why he covered his face rather than his privates. The rabbi replied, "I don't know about you, but in my congregation, it's my face they would recognize."

* * *

Everyone likes to have a good face and a good image before others. What is more important is not what others think about you but what you think about yourself.

Do you have a good self-image? Self-image results from how you see yourself, how others see you and how you perceive others see you.

It is important that you have a realistic image about yourself. Accept and love yourself as you are. Be happy with yourself. If you have a positive self-image, people are more likely to see you as a positive, capable person. A positive self-image enhances your physical, mental, emotional, social, and spiritual wellness.

"A strong, positive self-image is the best possible preparation for success in life." – Dr. Joyce Brothers.

"A man cannot be comfortable without his own approval."
– Mark Twain

Themes: Self-image, Recognition, Minister, Rabbi, Priest,
Positive, Hike, Swim, Ladies, Face.

62. THE GOOD SAMARITAN

A Sunday school teacher was telling her class the story of
the Good Samaritan, in which a man was beaten, robbed and
left for dead. She described the situation in vivid detail so her
students would catch the drama. Then, she asked the class,
"If you saw a person lying on the roadside, all wounded and
bleeding, what would you do?"

A thoughtful little girl broke the hushed silence, "I think I'd
throw up."

* * *

Your action or reaction depends on what you perceive. And
your perception is influenced by your conscience. If you are
always thinking about serving others, acts of kindness will
come naturally to you.

There is so much joy in giving than receiving. When you are
connected to others, serve others without expectations in return
you experience joy.

Just simple acts of kindness and caring for others can cure
your loneliness and give you a great experience of joy. Look for
occasions to increase your joy by caring for each other.

"The best way to find yourself is to lose yourself in the service of others." – Mahatma Gandhi

"The highest form of worship is the worship of unselfish Christian service. The greatest form of praise is the sound of consecrated feet seeking out the lost and helpless." – Billy Graham

Themes: Service, Love, Charity, Good Samaritan, Joy, Giving, Kindness, Perception.

63. PROGRAMMING CONTEST

Jesus and Satan get into an argument as to who is the better programmer. This goes on for a few hours until they come to an agreement to hold a contest, with God as the judge.

They seat themselves at their computers and begin. They type furiously, lines of code streaming up the screen, for several hours straight. Seconds before the end of the competition, a bolt of lightning strikes, and the electricity is gone. Moments later, the power is restored, and God announces that the contest is over.

He asks Satan to show what he has come up with. Satan is visibly upset, and cries, "I have nothing. I lost it all when the power went out."

"Very well, then," says God, "let us see if Jesus fared any better."

Jesus enters a command, and the screen comes to life in vivid display, the voices of an angelic choir pour forth from the speakers. Satan is astonished.

He stutters, "B-b-but how? I lost everything, yet Jesus' program is intact. How did he do it?"

God smiled all-knowingly, "Jesus saves."

* * *

"Jesus saves" is a popular slogan on bumper stickers. Jesus became incarnate, lived our lives, suffered, died and rose to life that we might be saved. It is our total faith in Him that will bring about our salvation.

The Bible says that every person who has ever lived has sinned. Because we have sinned against an infinite God, an infinite God has to save us. Our God loved us so much that He Himself became one of us to save us. He did not love us from far. He took on our human form to show what true love is. Develop a personal relationship with Him and be assured of eternal life.

"Three things are necessary for our salvation: to know what we ought to believe; to know what we ought to desire; to know what we ought to do." – Thomas Aquinas

"Faith in the Lord Jesus Christ is the foundation upon which sincere and meaningful repentance must be built. If we truly seek to put away sin, we must first look to Him who is the Author of our salvation." – Ezra Taft Benson

Themes: Salvation, Jesus Christ, Bible, God, Satan, Programmer, Savior.

64. POLICE AT THE LOCAL BAR

A routine police patrol parked outside a local neighborhood bar. Late in the evening the officer noticed a man leaving the bar so intoxicated he could barely walk. The man stumbled around the parking lot for a few minutes with the officer quietly observing. After what seemed an eternity and trying his keys on five different vehicles he managed to find his own car into which he fell. He was there for a few minutes as a number of other patrons left the bar and drove off.

Finally, he started the car, switched the wipers on and off (it was a dry night), flicked the hazard flasher, tooted the horn and then switched on the lights. He moved the vehicle forward a few inches, reversed a little and remained stationary for a few more minutes as more patrons left in their vehicles. At last he pulled out of the parking lot and started driving slowly down the street. The police officer, having patiently waited all this time, now started up his patrol car, put on the flashing lights, promptly pulled the man over and carried out a Breathalyzer test. To his amazement, the Breathalyzer indicated no evidence of the man having consumed alcohol at all.

Dumbfounded, the officer said, "I'll have to ask you to accompany me to the police station, apparently this equipment is broken.

"I doubt it," said the man, "Tonight I'm the designated decoy."

* * *

Appearance can be deceptive. There are so many ways you can be lured and trapped today. There are teasers and trickery everywhere.

All that glitters is not gold is an old saying, that means not everything that looks precious or true turns out to be so. Don't be fooled by what you see on the surface. Good observation leads to better judgment. Take time to see, judge and act.

"You can fool some of the people all the time, and all the people some of the time, but you cannot fool all of the people all the time." – Abraham Lincoln

"Deception may give us what we want for the present, but it will always take it away in the end." – Rachel Hawthome

Themes: Drinking and Driving, Appearance, Deception, Fraud, Judgment.

65. DRIVER AND POLICE OFFICER

A police officer pulls over a speeding car. The officer says, I clocked you at 80 miles per hour, sir." The driver says, "Gee, officer I had it on cruise control at 60, perhaps your radar gun needs calibrating."

Not looking up from her knitting the wife says: "Now don't be silly dear, you know that this car doesn't have cruise control." As the officer writes out the ticket, the driver looks over at his wife and growls, "Can't you please keep your mouth shut for once?" The wife smiles demurely and says, "You should be thankful your radar detector went off when it did." As the officer makes out the second ticket for the illegal radar detector unit, the man glowers at his wife and says through clenched teeth, "Darn it, woman, can't you keep your mouth shut?"

The officer frowns and says, "And I notice that you're not wearing your seat belt, sir. That's an automatic $75 fine."

The driver says, "Yeah, well, you see officer, I had it on, but took it off when you pulled me over so that I could get my license out of my back pocket." The wife says, "Now, dear, you know very well that you didn't have your seat belt on. You never wear your seat belt when you're driving. "And as the police officer is writing out the third ticket the driver turns to his wife and barks, "Why don't you please shut up?"

The officer looks over at the woman and asks, "Does your husband always talk to you this way, Ma'am?"

"Only when he's been drinking."

* * *

Honesty is the best policy is an old proverb. It may seem advantage to tell a lie but it is best to be honest. Only through honesty you can prove to others that you are trustworthy and gain their respect.

Honesty and truth can be hard. Sometimes people do not want to hear the truth and that can lead to "lip service" and being a charade.

Researchers say that white lies may seem harmless at the time, but bending the truth can actually cause physical and mental health.

The greatest advantage of speaking the truth is that you don't have to remember what you said.

"Honesty is the first chapter in the book of wisdom." – Thomas Jefferson

"Honesty is the best policy. If I lose mine honor, I lose myself." – William Shakespeare

Themes: Honesty, Trustworthy, Morality, Truth, Pretense, Police Officer, Drunk Driving.

66. THE REQUEST OF THE DYING PRIEST

An old priest was dying. He sent a message to two members of the parish, an IRS agent and the diocesan lawyer, to come to the rectory.

When they arrived, they were ushered up to his bedroom. As they entered the room, the priest held out his hands and motioned for them to sit on each side of the bed. The priest grasped their hands, sighed contentedly, smiled and stared at the ceiling.

For a time, no one said anything. Both the IRS agent and lawyer were touched and flattered that the old priest would ask them to be with him during his final moment. They were also puzzled because the priest had never given any indication that he particularly liked either one of them.

Finally, the Lawyer asked, "Father, why did you ask the two of us to come?"

The old priest mustered up some strength, then said weakly, "Jesus died between two thieves, and that's how I want to go, too!"

* * *

Jesus said: "I am the resurrection and the life; whoever believes in me, even if he dies, will live, and everyone who lives and believes in me will never die." (John 11:25)

You don't have to be afraid of death because it is only a passage from earthly life to eternal life. After death, you will be in the presence of our loving God, angels and saints.

Those who have had near death experience tell us that life continues to exist after death and that they are in a state of pure joy. All world religions believe in life after death. That is why saints embrace death joyfully. Remember that life here on earth is a parenthesis in eternity.

"We are not human beings having a spiritual experience. We are spiritual beings having a human experience." – Teilhard de Chardin

"The fear of death follows from the fear of life. A man who lives fully is prepared to die at any time." – Mark Twain

Theme: Life, Death, Resurrection, Heaven, Priest, Lawyer, IRS, Eternity, Fear, Near Death Experience, Life After Death.

67. INTERESTING DOG NAMES

A girl was visiting her blonde friend, who had acquired two new dogs, and asked her what their names were. The blonde responded by saying that one was named *Rolex* and the other *Timex.*

Her friend said, "Whoever heard of someone naming dogs like that? "Hello," answered the blond. "They're watch dogs."

* * *

"Watch and pray that you may not undergo the test" (Matthew 26:41). Jesus is asking us to be vigilant and on guard, fully awake, aware, attentive and laser focused. We need to be in a state of readiness always because Christ will come again when we least expect Him.

Christ's coming can be at the end of the world or at our death. If you are fully prepared to go and to be with God eternally, you do not have to be anxious. You have to be like the fire fighters or police officers who are prepared to go on the mission immediately when they are called.

What you could do now is to be at peace with God and everyone. Take time to reconcile if you have offended anyone or God.

"Watch your thoughts, they become words. Watch your words, they become actions. Watch your actions, they become habits. Watch your habits, they become your character. Watch your character, it becomes your destiny." – Anonymous

"The trouble is, you think you have time." – Buddha

Themes: Watchfulness, Time, Death, Peace, Reconciliation, Alertness, Vigilance, Preparedness.

68. Aid to the Homeless

I was walking down the street when I was accosted by a particularly dirty and shabby-looking homeless man who asked me for a couple of dollars for dinner.

I took out my wallet, extracted ten dollars and asked, "If I give you this money, will you buy some beer with it instead?"

"No, I had to stop drinking years ago," the homeless man replied.

"Will you use it to gamble instead of buying food?" I asked.

"No, I don't gamble," the homeless man said. "I need everything I can get just to stay alive."

"Will you spend this on greens fees at a golf course instead of food?" I asked.

"Are you nuts!" replied the homeless man. "I haven't played golf in 20 years."

"Will you spend the money on a woman in the red light district instead of food?" I asked.

"What disease would I get for ten lousy bucks?!!" exclaimed the homeless man.

"Well," I said, "I'm not going to give you the money. Instead, I'm going to take you home for a terrific dinner cooked by my wife Beverly."

The homeless man was astounded. "Won't your wife be furious with you for doing that? I know I'm dirty, and I probably smell pretty disgusting."

I replied, "That's okay. I just want her to see what a man looks like who's given up beer, gambling, golf, and sex."

* * *

Appearances often deceive. Yet we often judge and evaluate persons just based on outward appearance. Some people give a lot of importance to facial make-up or building the façade.

What is important is the interior. Externals are often only camouflage. But the internal state of our being will be manifested externally too.

Appearances make impressions but it is the personality that makes an impact. A beautiful appearance will last a few decades, but a beautiful personality will last a lifetime.

"Don't judge the book by the cover." It is very easy to fall into the trap of looking only at the surface of people, things, and ideas without taking the time and effort to delve deeper into them.

"Appearance and reality are polar opposites." Leif Ericsson Leo Vaness

"Do not judge by appearances; a rich heart may be under a poor coat." Scottish proverb

Themes: Appearance, Façade, Externals, Internals, Lent, Self Sacrifice.

69. SHOPPING WINDOW CURTAINS

A blonde enters a store that sells curtains. She tells the salesman, "I would like to buy a pair of pink curtains."

The salesman assures her that they have a large selection of pink curtains. He shows her several patterns, but the blonde seems to have a hard time choosing.

Finally she selects a lovely pink floral print. The salesman then asks what size curtains she needs.

The blonde promptly replies, "Fifteen inches."

"Fifteen inches?" asked the salesman. "That sounds very small - what room are they for?"

The blonde tells him that they aren't for a room, but they are for her computer monitor.

The surprised salesman replies, "But miss, computers do not need curtains!"

The blond says, "Hello! I've got Windows!"

* * *

Some people have all their curtains closed in their homes all the time. They miss the natural light and beautiful scenery outside their home. In the same way people who are closed up within themselves do not enjoy the bright world around them. They miss the beauty of relating with the world around them.

"No man is an island." We are born to live with others in society. When we have good interpersonal relationship, our very lives will be enhanced. For a healthy relationship, we have to overlook the faults and failures of others. Try to see the good in others.

"To touch the soul of another human being is to walk on holy ground." - Stephen R. Covey

"True love is a process of co-creation in which neither feels ownership or superiority. Jealousy is a highly destructive force for love and relationships." – Jonathan Lockwood Huie

Themes: Computers, Blonde, Shopping, Windows, Openness, Relationship, Society,

70. WHAT'S FOR SUPPER?

An elderly gentleman of 85 feared his wife was getting hard of hearing. So one day he called her doctor to make an appointment to have her hearing checked. The doctor made an appointment for a hearing test in two weeks, and meanwhile there's a simple informal test the husband could do to give the doctor some idea of the state of her problem.

"Here's what you do," said the doctor, "start out about 40 feet away from her, and in a normal conversational speaking tone see if she hears you. If not, go to 30 feet, then 20 feet, and so on until you get a response."

That evening, the wife is in the kitchen cooking dinner, and he's in the living room. He says to himself, "I'm about 40 feet away, let's see what happens."

Then in a normal tone he asks, ‹Honey, what's for supper?" No response.

So the husband moved to the other end of the room, about 30 feet from his wife and repeats, "Honey, what's for supper?" Still no response.

Next he moves into the dining room where he is about 20 feet from his wife and asks, "Honey, what's for supper?" Again he gets no response so he walks up to the kitchen door, only 10 feet away. "Honey, what's for supper?"

Again there is no response, so he walks right up behind her. "Honey, what's for supper?"

"Damn it Earl, for the fourth time, chicken!"

* * *

It is easy to find fault with others while we are oblivious of the same fault in us. In a way, when we are full of ourselves, we are blinded. We often find the very limitation that we have to be a limitation of others. In psychiatry 'projection' is a defense mechanism by which your own traits and emotions are attributed to someone else.

When you point a finger at someone, you should remember that three of your fingers are pointing at yourself.

Do you recognize and admit your mistakes and faults? Or do you find yourself blaming others often? Don't worry about what people say behind your back, they are the people who are finding faults in your life instead of fixing the faults in their own life.

Recognizing and owning up responsibility for your mistakes and faults is important to your growth and well-being.

"Let none find fault with others. Let none see the omissions and commissions of others. But let one see one's own acts done and undone." – The Buddha

"Don't find fault, find a remedy." – Henry Ford

Themes: Judgment, Criticism, Condemnation, Faults, Mistakes, Projection, Blame.

71. EMPATHY OF A CHILD

While I sat in the reception area of my doctor's office, a woman rolled an elderly man in a wheelchair into the room. As she went to the receptionist's desk, the man sat there, alone and silent.

Just as I was thinking I should make small talk with him, a little boy slipped off his mother's lap and walked over to the wheelchair.

Placing his hand on the man's, he said, "I know how you feel. My mom makes me ride in the stroller too."

* * *

Empathy is the ability to understand and share the feeling of another person. This skill can lead you to great success personally and professionally. This when practiced will improve your interpersonal relationship. This can also give you profound inner joy. If you are empathetic you will treat others the way you want to be treated. You will look out for occasions to take care of the needs of people around you.

When people speak to you, listen attentively and respond

lovingly. Look at people's faces and show that you are interested when they are talking to you. Be slow to make judgment. Put yourself in the shoes of the other. Try to see with the eyes of another, listen with the ears of another and feel with the heart of another.

"When you show deep empathy toward others, their defensive energy goes down, and positive energy replaces it. That's when you can get more creative in solving problems." – Stephen Covey

"When you start to develop your powers of empathy and imagination, the whole world opens up to you." – Susan Sarandon

Themes: Empathy, Sympathy, Understanding, Love, Compassion, Relationship, Mother, Mom, Child, Doctor's Office, Elderly, Wheelchair, Stroller.

72. THE ABSCONDING HUSBAND

A man left work one Friday afternoon, but instead of going home, he stayed out the entire weekend, hunting with the boys and spending his entire paycheck.

When he finally appeared at home on Sunday night, he was confronted by his very angry wife and was barraged for nearly two hours with a tirade about his actions.

Finally his wife stopped the nagging and simply said to him: "How would you like it if you didn't see me for two or three days?"

To which he replied, "That would be fine with me."

Monday went by and he didn't see his wife. Tuesday and Wednesday came and went and he didn't see her.

On Thursday, the swelling went down just enough where he could see her a little out of the corner of his left eye.

* * *

We live in a world that is blessed by existence of fast communication systems. Communication is enhanced by the worldwide postal system, telephone network, Internet, emails etc.

In spite of all the facilities do we communicate enough? The better the communication the better the clarity and understanding among family members. Due to poor or lack of communications marriages are broken, relationships wrecked, friendships are ruined.

Free and frank conversation is essential for healthy family life. It is important to have a sense of trust and confidence for effective communication. We need to listen more and to talk less. Listen to what the other is not saying.

"Tell me and I'll forget. Show me and I might remember. Involve me and I will understand." – Benjamin Franklin

"Communication to a relationship is like oxygen to life. Without it…it dies." – Tony Gaskins

Themes: Communication, Conversation, Dialogue, Family life, Interaction, Marriage, Matrimony, Husband, Wife, Dispute.

73. Fully Equipped Campground

A very proper lady began planning a week's camping vacation for her and her Baptist Church group. She wrote to a campground for reservations.

She wanted to make sure that the campground was fully equipped and modern, but couldn't bring herself to write the word "toilet" in her letter. So, she decided on the old-fashioned term "Bathroom Commode." Once written down she still was not comfortable. Finally she decided on the abbreviation "B.C." and wrote, "Does your campground have its own 'B.C.'?"

When the campground owner received the letter, he couldn't figure out what she meant by "B.C." He showed it to several of the campers, one of whom suggested the lady was obviously referring to a Baptist Church since there was a letterhead on the paper which referred to a Baptist Church. So he sent this reply.

Dear Madam:

The B.C. is located nine miles from the campground in a beautiful grove of trees. I admit it is quite a distance if you are in the habit of going regularly. No doubt you will be pleased to know that it will seat 350 people at one time, and it is open on Tuesday, Thursday, and Sunday of each week. Some folks like to take their lunch and make a day of it. The acoustics are very good, so everyone can hear even the quietest passages. It may interest you to know that my daughter met her husband there. We are also having a fund-raiser to purchase new seats, as the old ones have holes in them. Unfortunately, my wife is ill and has not been able to attend regularly. It's been a good six months since she last went. It pains her very much not to be able to go more often. As we grow older, it seems to be more of an effort, especially in cold weather. Perhaps I could accompany you the first time you go, sit with you, and introduce you to all the other folks who will be there.

I look forward to your visit. We offer a very friendly campground.

* * *

Straightforward would mean free from ambiguity. It is simple and uncomplicated. The trouble starts when you are not frank and honest with yourself and those around you. You are to live a life without concealment or deception.

Straightforwardness is vital for good relationship and smooth living. People appreciate those who are frank and honest. A certain amount of simplicity will help in this regard.

"If you can't explain it simply, you don't understand it well enough." – Albert Einstein

"Be yourself; everyone else is already taken." – Oscar Wilde

Themes: Straightforwardness, Honesty, Frankness, Ambiguity, Simplicity.

74. Facial Makeup

Little Johnny watched, fascinated, as his mother smoothed cold cream on her face. "Why do you do that, Mommy?" he asked.

"To make myself beautiful," said his mother, who then began removing the cream with a tissue.

"What's the matter?" asked Little Johnny. "Giving up?"

* * *

Persistence always pays rich dividends. Thomas Edison who invented the light bulb when asked if he was not discouraged with the numerous experiments that failed, replied: "I have learned that in a thousand ways it doesn't work."

Some people succeed in spite of handicaps. Others succeed because of them. The truth is, our problems help to make us what we are. Those who suffer often learn the value of compassion. Those who struggle often learn perseverance. And those who fall down often teach others how to rise again. Our troubles can shape us in ways a carefree existence cannot.

A river cuts through a rock not because of its power, but its persistence. Never underestimate the power of persistence.

"Great works are performed not by strength but by perseverance." - Samuel Johnson

"With ordinary talent and extraordinary perseverance, all things are attainable." – Thomas Foxwell Buxton

Themes: Perseverance, Persistence, Determination, Diligence, Tenacity, Giving up, Problems.

75. BUSY STREET CROSSING

Paddy was in New York. He was patiently waiting, and watching the traffic cop on a busy street crossing. The cop stopped the flow of traffic and shouted, "Okay pedestrians." Then he'd allow the traffic to pass.

He'd done this several times, and Paddy still stood on the sidewalk. After the cop had shouted "Pedestrians" for the tenth time, Paddy went over to him and said, "Is it not about time ye let the Catholics across?"

* * *

There is a time for everything if you are well organized. In the world there are many disparities but all the people have same amount of time each day. Time is a precious commodity. Even if one is rich, one cannot buy extra time. You have to be good stewards of time. Use wisely the limited time that you have.

Avoid wasting time by being a good manager of time. Plan your activity, plan your day, week and month and remember to keep the plan. The quality of your life depends on how you spend your time. As good and responsible stewards of time, give some of it generously to God.

"It's not enough to be busy, so are the ants. The question is, what are we busy about?" – Henry David Thoreau

"Guard well your spare moments. They are like uncut diamonds. Discard them and their value will never be known. Improve them and they will become the brightest gems in a useful life." – Ralph Waldo Emerson

Themes: Time, Time Management, Day, Week, Spare Time, Diamonds, Catholics, Pedestrians, Presbyterians, Cop.

76. RESOURCEFUL BIBLE

A little boy opened the big, old family Bible with fascination and looked at the old pages as he turned them.

Suddenly, something fell out of the Bible, and he picked it up and looked at it closely. It was an old leaf from a tree that had been pressed in between the pages.

"What have you got there, dear?" his mother asked.

With astonishment in his voice, the young boy answered: "I think I just found Adam's suit!"

* * *

The Bible is the number one best seller in the world. The word "Bible" comes from the Greek word "biblia" meaning "books". In the Bible we find God's love expressed in words. It is God's love letter to us. Therein we have the direction for our life. So Bible study is a necessity, not a luxury.

A father was approached by his small son who told him proudly, "I know what the Bible means!" His father smiled and replied, "What do you mean, you 'know' what the Bible means?" The son replied, "I do know!" "Okay, said his father. "So, son, what does the Bible mean?" "That's easy Daddy, It stands for 'Basic Information Before Leaving Earth.'"

"For the word of God is living and active (Hebrews 4:12) and "has power to build you up" (Acts 20:32). It will empower you. Reading and studying the scripture is the duty and responsibility for all believers.

"A thorough knowledge of the Bible is worth more than a college education." – Theodore Roosevelt

"Ignorance of the Scriptures is ignorance of Christ." – St. Jerome

Themes: Bible, Scriptures, Basic Information, God's Love, Inspiration, Best Seller, Books, Little Boy, Mother, Adam.

77. SOLO-HELICOPTER FLIGHT

A blonde pilot decided she wanted to learn how to fly a helicopter. She went to the airport, but the only one available was a solo-helicopter.

The Instructor figured he could let her go up alone since she was already a pilot for small planes and he could instruct her via radio.

So up the blonde went. She reached 1,000 feet and everything was going smoothly. She reached 2,000 feet. The blonde and the Instructor kept talking via radio. Everything was running smoothly.

At 3,000 feet the helicopter suddenly came down quickly! It skimmed the top of some trees and crash landed in the woods.

The Instructor jumped into his jeep and rushed out to see if the blonde was okay.

As he reached the edge of the woods, the blonde was walking out. "What happened?" the Instructor asked. "All was going so well until you reached 3,000 feet. What happened then?"

"Well," began the blonde, "It was getting too cold. So I turned off the ceiling fan."

* * *

Self-reliant persons are the ones who believe in themselves and in their abilities. Self-confidence helps you to progress and achieve. Self-assurance will lead you to greater heights. Confidence comes naturally with success but success comes only to those who are confident.

Self-confidence is the most attractive quality a person can have. How can anyone see how great you are if you can't see it yourself?

However, it is great to put your trust in others and seek help when needed. Trust and confidence can bring you closer to others. That can pave the way for friendship. "No man is an island." You need companionship in life. When you have good friends, you can easily ask for help and get good direction.

"I am not what has happened to me. I am what I choose to become." – Carl Jung

"Don't let what you can't do stop you from doing what you can do." – John Wooden

Themes: Self-reliance, Self-assurance, Self-confidence, Trust, Self-reliance, Confidence, Overconfidence, Foolishness, Instructor, Helicopter, Pilot, Blonde.

78. BAD WEATHER AT THE GOLF COURSE

A pastor, an avid golfer, was once taking part in a local tournament. As he was preparing to tee off, the organizer of the tournament approached him and pointed to the dark, threatening storm clouds which were gathering.

"Preacher," the organizer said, "I trust you'll see to it that the weather won't turn bad on us."

The pastor shook his head. "Sorry," he replied. "I'm in sales, not in management!"

* * *

There are some things beyond your control. You do not have the power or authority to check or restrain everything. Leave them in the hands of God and He will take care of them. The Bible never once says, "Figure it out." But over and over it says, "Trust God." He is already got it all figured out.

You do not have to manage everything. Instead trust in God. There is freedom in recognizing you are not in charge of everything. There is a higher source or intelligence that controls everything that is in the universe. Everything that happens has a purpose and that is meant to be.

Look back and thank God. Look forward and trust God. He closes doors no one can open and He opens doors no one can close. When we put our problems in God's hands, he puts His peace in our hearts.

True freedom and joy comes when you can be grateful for the adversities that happen in your life.

"Blessed is the man who trusts in the Lord whose confidence is in Him." Jeremiah 17:7

"Sometimes your only available transportation is a leap of faith." - Margaret Shepard

Themes: Sales, Management, Faith, Trust, God, Freedom, Joy, Abandonment, Power, Bible, Weather, Golf, Preacher, Pastor.

79. PUBLIC SERVANT

"Give me a sentence about a public servant," said a teacher.

A small boy wrote: "The fireman came down the ladder pregnant."

The teacher took the lad aside to correct him. "Don't you know what pregnant means?" she asked.

"Sure," said the young boy confidently. "It means carrying a child."

* * *

Public servants do service for the community or people as a whole. Their jobs can be very tedious and challenging. The firefighters and police personnel have to be always in a state of preparedness for they do not know when their services will be required.

Be ready to serve others. Good leadership is through service. How wonderful this world would be if everyone gave up their egoism and thought about the welfare of others. You should be willing to work to lighten the burden of others.

Ask yourself: "How may I serve?" and not "What is in it for me?"

"At the end of life we will not be judged by how many diplomas we have received, how much money we have made, how many great things we have done. We will be judged by "I was hungry, and you gave me something to eat, I was naked and you clothed me. I was homeless, and you took me in." – Blessed Mother Teresa.

"No one is useless in this world who lightens the burdens of another." – Charles Dickens

Themes: Public servant, Service, Love, Egoism, Leader Teacher, Fireman, Pregnancy.

80. JUST A SECOND

Jamie: "God, how long is a million years to you?"

God: "It is but a second Jamie."

Jamie: "God, how much is a million dollars to you?"

God: "It is but a penny to me."

Jamie: "God, can I have a penny?"

God: "Just a second!"

* * *

What is your notion of God? God is sometimes portrayed as an angry tyrant just waiting to punish us. People who believe in the "wrath of God" are awaiting punishment.

Some others portray God as a benign buddy. He is looked upon as a gracious guy who asks you to be just good.

God is infinite. God cannot be fitted into your fists or into your prayer books. He is the master creator of the universe.

God is a God of love. He is ever close to you. And He dwells in your hearts. You are free and so you can refuse the love of God but you can never lose the love of God. You need not be afraid of where you're going when you know God is going with you.

"He who kneels before God can stand before anyone." – Anonymous

"God gave us the gift of life; it is up to us to give ourselves the gift of living well." - Voltaire

Themes: God, Time, Money, Love, Immortality, Eternity, Buddy, Fear.

81. KNOWLEDGE OF THE WITNESS

A small town prosecuting attorney called his first witness to the stand in a trial - a grandmotherly, elderly woman. He approached her and asked, "Mrs. Jones, do you know me?"

She responded, "Why, yes, I do know you Mr. Williams. I've known you since you were a young boy. And frankly, you've been a big disappointment to me. You lie, you cheat on your wife, you manipulate people and talk about them behind their backs. You think you're a rising big shot when you haven't the brains to realize you never will amount to anything more than a two-bit paper pusher. Yes, I know you."

The lawyer was stunned. Not knowing what else to do he pointed across the room and asked, "Mrs. Williams, do you know the defense attorney?" She again replied, "Why, yes I do. I've known Mr. Bradley since he was a youngster, too. I used to baby-sit him for his parents. And he, too, has been a real disappointment to me. He's lazy, bigoted, and he has a drinking problem. The man can't build a normal relationship with anyone and his law practice is one of the worst in the entire state. Not to mention he cheated on his wife with three different women. Yes, I know him." The defense attorney was also surprised and shocked.

At this point, the judge brought the courtroom to silence and called both counselors to the bench. In a very quiet voice, he said with menace, "If either of you bastards asks her if she knows me, you'll be jailed for contempt!"

* * *

There are some people who pretend to know it all. They seem to know everything about everyone. Their verbose gossip has no end.

In the eagerness to show off their information, they cut and slice people. They just go on with character assassination.

The listeners have to take in these types of bombastic monologues with a pinch of salt. Needless to say that they are pompous and self-righteous.

"Said the self-righteous preacher, 'what, in your judgment is the greatest sin in the world?' 'That of the person who sees other human beings as sinners, said the Master.'" – Anthony de Mello

"Be righteous without being self-righteous." – Ahmed Rehab

Themes: Self-righteous, Complacent, Hypocritical, Gossip, Pompous person, Pride, Straightforward.

82. HE WAS PRESIDENT

A father noticed that his son was spending way too much time on the Internet.

In an effort to motivate the boy into focusing more attention on his schoolwork, the father said to his son, "When Abe Lincoln was your age, he was studying books by the light of the fireplace."

The son replied, "Dad, when Lincoln was your age, he was The President of The United States!!!"

* * *

You can become whatever you want in life if you have the courage to pursue them. Have a burning desire. Make the burning desire into goals. If you have a goal and you are willing to work hard to achieve, you will achieve whatever you want. Nothing should deter you from achieving your goal.

It is never too late to have a dream and make it a reality. Have passion and motivation to achieve your goal. Hard work will reach you there.

"You're never given a dream without also being given the power to make it true." – Richard Bach

"Happy are those who dream dreams and are ready to pay the price to make them come true." – Leo Jozef Suenens

Themes: Father, Son, Dad, Goal, Dreams, Desires, Passion, Motivation, Hard Work.

83. TEST TO ENTER HEAVEN

The husband died and reached heaven. St. Peter received him at the gates of heaven and told him: "There is a little test that you have to pass to be admitted into heaven. Just spell the word 'love'." He spelled it correctly and he was permitted to enter into heaven.

Just then Peter got a call and he had to leave the gates. So Peter asked the new arrival to man the gates for a few minutes.

Then his wife reached the gates, too. So the husband said to his wife: "There is a little test that you have to pass to be admitted into heaven."

"What is it?," she asked.

He said: "Spell 'Czechoslovakia."

* * *

"Familiarity breeds contempt." It is hard for some to love people who are close. They enjoy making life miserable for them.

When there is true love, one would be eager to reach out. You find happiness when you make the life happy for others.

The measure with which we give, with the same measure we will receive.

Forgiveness is vital for long lasting marriage. Because you're human, because you are made up of flesh and blood, you can hurt each other. There can be little quarrels, misunderstandings and small exchange of words. When they occur do reconcile, forgive and make peace. A happy marriage is the union of two good forgivers.

"Forgiveness is the fragrance that the violet shed on the heel that crushed it." – Mark Twain

"Do not let the sun set on your anger." Ephesians 4:26

Themes: Familiarity, Marriage, Love, Happiness, Forgiveness, Hurt, Anger, Reconciliation, peace, Test, Punishment.

84. PICTURES OF BIBLE STORY

Susie asked her Sunday school class to draw pictures of their favorite Bible stories. She was puzzled by Jimmy's picture which showed four people on an airplane, so she asked him which story it was meant to represent. "The flight to Egypt," said Jimmy.

"I see . . . and that must be Mary, Joseph, and Baby Jesus," Susie said. "But who's the fourth person?"

"Oh, that's Pontius the Pilot."

* * *

Interpretation is very personal and subjective. Every artist has a way of expressing his or her thought or embodying his or her conception of nature.

Our interpretation is based on our knowledge and influenced by our environment. We are the result of the genes we have inherited and the environment in which we have been brought up. We cannot change our heredity but we can change our environment.

When the door of happiness closes, another opens. But often times you look so long at the closed door that you don't see the one which has been opened for you.

Children have their ways to find solutions to problems and challenges. They have a free flow of imagination. The thinking pattern of adults is curtailed and controlled by their knowledge and experience.

Creativity and imagination are for all. Think out of the box and be prepared to have a new mindset.

"Creativity is intelligence having fun." – Albert Einstein

"A creative man is motivated by the desire to achieve, not by the desire to beat others." – Ayn Rand

Themes: Creativity, Imagination, Challenges, Problems, Discouragement, Bible, Bible Stories, Happiness, Holy Family, Interpretation, Hereditary, Environment

85. The Dumped Wife

After 17 years of marriage, a man dumped his wife for a younger woman. The downtown luxury apartment was in his name and he wanted to remain there with his new love so he asked the wife to move out and then he would buy her another place.

The wife agreed to this, but asked that she be given three days on her own in the house, to pack up her things.

While he was gone, the first day she lovingly put her personal belongings into boxes and crates and suitcases.

On the second day, she had the movers come and collect her things.

On the third day, she sat down for the last time at their candlelit dining table, soft music playing in the background, and feasted on a pound of shrimp and a bottle of Chardonnay.

When she had finished, she went into each room and deposited a few of the resulting shrimp shells into the hollow of the curtain rods. She then cleaned up the kitchen and left.

The husband came back, with his new girl, and all was bliss for the first few days. Then it started; slowly but surely. Clueless, the man could not explain why the place smelled so bad.

They tried everything; cleaned and mopped and aired the place out. Vents were checked for dead rodents, carpets were steam cleaned, air fresheners were hung everywhere. Exterminators were brought in, the carpets were replaced, and on it went.

Finally, they could take it no more and decided to move. The moving company arrived and did a very professional packing job, taking everything to their new home ... including the curtain rods.

* * *

New shoots come up if only the plant is cut down because the roots still remain. If the problem has to be eliminated the root cause of the problem should be eliminated.

Don't you sometimes try to solve the problems by just covering it up? But the lid will easily be pushed out. Find the source of the evil and eradicate it from there.

"The evil that men do lives after them; the good is oft interred with their bones." – William Shakespeare

"An evil person is like a dirty window, they never let the light shine through." – William Makepeace Thackeray

Themes: Problems, Evil, Wickedness, Root cause, Marriage, Home, Husband, Wife, Divorce.

86. KILLER WHALE SHOW

At Sea World, the little boy firmly refused to see the show featuring Shamu the killer whale, but he wouldn't tell why. No amount of discussion could get him to change his mind.

Later, when the family got home, they discovered the reason for his reluctance. An aunt had told him how exciting the show would be because "...they choose children from the audience to feed Shamu."

* * *

The purpose of language is to communicate. But it can also cause misunderstanding. Misunderstanding is an understanding of something that is not correct. Sometimes, the idea communicated may not be clear enough. The problem could be the fault of the communicator.

Misunderstanding can mean putting the wrong interpretation on something. Misunderstandings can also be caused by lack of openness of the listener. When you are not open you try to understand the way you want.

Many of the problems in the world would disappear if we were to talk to each other instead of about each other.

"The single biggest problem in communication is the illusion that it has taken place." – George Bernard Shaw

"The most important thing in communication is hearing what isn't said." – Peter Drucker

Themes: Misunderstanding, Misinterpretation, Controversy, Misconception, Communication, Whales, Children, Family.

87. YOUR REWARD IN HEAVEN

The 85 year old couple, and had been married for sixty years. Though they were far from rich, they managed to get by because they were careful about every penny they spent.

Though not young, they were both in very good health, largely due to the wife's insistence on healthy foods and exercise for the last decade.

One day, their good health didn't help when they went on a rare vacation and their plane crashed, sending them off to Heaven. They reached the pearly gates, and St. Peter escorted them inside. He took them to a beautiful mansion, furnished in gold and fine silk, with a fully stocked kitchen and a waterfall in the master bath. A maid could be seen hanging their favorite clothes in the closet. They gasped in astonishment when he said, "Welcome to Heaven. This will be your home now."

The old man asked Peter how much all this was going to cost. "Why, nothing," Peter replied, "Remember, this is your reward in Heaven." The old man looked out of the window and right there he saw a championship golf course, finer and more beautiful than any ever built on Earth.

"What are the greens' fees?" grumbled the old man. "This is heaven," St. Peter replied. "You can play for free, every day." Next they went to the clubhouse and saw the lavish buffet lunch, with every imaginable cuisine laid out before them, from seafood to steaks to exotic desserts, free flowing beverages. "Don't even ask," said St. Peter to the man. "This is Heaven, it is all free for you to enjoy."

The old man looked around and glanced nervously at his wife. "Well, where are the low fat and low cholesterol foods, and the decaffeinated tea?" he asked. "That's the best part," St. Peter replied. "You can eat and drink as much as you like of whatever you like, and you will never get fat or sick ... this is Heaven!"

The old man pushed, "No gym to work out at?" "Not unless you want to," was the answer. "No testing my sugar or blood pressure or ..." "Never again. All you do here is enjoy yourself."

The old man glared at his wife and said, "You and your bran muffins. We could have been here ten years ago!"

* * *

You can make heaven or hell wherever we want. Others cannot make that for you. You are responsible for your own happiness. A little faith will bring your soul to heaven, but a lot of faith will bring heaven to your soul.

Heaven is not for people who are better than the rest but for people who sincerely try to become better than they already are.

Do not fear death because the life after that in heaven is beautiful, too. But that depends on how you live now.

"Aim at heaven and you will get earth thrown in. Aim at earth and you get neither." – C.S. Lewis

"My home is in heaven, I'm just traveling through this world." – Billy Graham

Themes: Heaven, Hell, Sacrifices, Life, Death, Healthy Life.

88. A CHRISTIAN AND AN ATHEIST

There's a little old Christian lady living next door to an atheist. Every morning the lady comes out onto her front porch and shouts "Praise the Lord!

The atheist yells back, "There is no God".

She does this every morning with the same result. As time goes on the lady runs into financial difficulties and has trouble buying food. She goes out onto the porch and asks God for help with groceries, then says "Praise the

Lord".

The next morning she goes out onto the porch and there's the groceries she has asked for, of course she says "Praise the Lord".

The atheist jumps out from behind a bush and says, "Ha, I bought those groceries - there is no God".

The lady looks at him and smiles, she shouts "Praise the Lord, not only did you provide for me, Lord, you made Satan pay for the groceries!"

* * *

A positive person is a grateful person. You will recognize God and others and will affirm the role that they play.

A positive person is an optimistic person. That person will look at the glass and say "Oh, good! It's half full." While the pessimist will look at the same thing and say: "Oh, nuts! It's half empty."

Optimism is the foundation of courage. The best is yet to come.

What is your vision of the reality? You can't live a positive life with a negative mind. The entire water of the sea can't sink a ship unless it gets inside the ship. Similarly, negativity of the world can't put you down unless you allow it to get inside you.

"Optimism is the faith that leads to achievement. Nothing can be done without hope and confidence." - Helen Keller

"If you change the way you look at things, the things you look at change." – Dr. Wayne Dyer

Themes: Positive Attitude, Optimism, Vision, Atheist, Christian, God, Satan, Groceries, Reality.

89. WISH FULFILLED

A man exploring the ancient Pyramids of Egypt while on vacation stumbled across a secret room. He sneaked out from the tour group and explored the room. He found a dusty lamp and picked it up. While he wiped the dust off the lamp a genie appeared in a puff of smoke.

"For freeing me from my prison, I will grant you a wish, what will it be sir?"

The man thought for a moment, then said, "I want a spectacular job, a job that no man has ever succeeded at or has ever attempted to do."

"Allah Ka Zam!" said the genie. "You're now a housewife!"

* * *

Every job is noble. There is great dignity in working. Woman and man are to share the workload. Yet it is a fact that women do more of the house chores. Husbands often think that it is the wife's responsibility to do all the cooking and cleaning. Husbands too can do that type of job very well. If the work is shared, it does become light.

A woman was once asked: "What work do you do?" She replied: "I don't do any work, I am only a housewife." Isn't that a work? Husbands should realize that it is a work.

Nothing worth having comes easy. There will be obstacles, doubts, and mistakes but with hard work there are no limits.

How do we view work in general? Do we realize that whatever we do contributes to make this world a better place?

"The only way to do great work is to love what you do." Steve Jobs

"There is no substitute for hard work." – Thomas Edison

Themes: Dignity of Labor, Work, Man, Women, Wife, Husband, Duty, Responsibility, Housewife, Equality.

90. CHOOSING HYMNS

A pastor explained to his congregation that the church was in need of some extra money, so he asked them to consider being more than generous. He promised them that whoever gave the most money that day would be allowed to pick three hymns. After the offering plates were passed around, the pastor glanced down and noticed that someone had graciously offered a $1,000 bill.

He was so excited that he immediately shared his joy with his congregation and said he'd like to personally thank the one who placed the money in the plate. A very quiet, elderly, lady in the back of the church shyly raised her hand. The pastor asked her to come to the front, so she slowly made her way towards him. The pastor told her how wonderful it was that she had given so generously, and in thanks he asked her to pick out three hymns.

Her eyes brightened as she looked over the congregation. She pointed out to the three very handsome men in the church and said, "I'll take him, and him, and him!"

* * *

Hymn or him? Hymns are composed to help you pray better. When one sings, one prays twice – so said the great Saint Augustine. Singing brings out the feelings and emotions. Bring the entire being to God in praying and singing. Praise God from whom all the blessings follow.

It is only natural to be attracted to handsome men or beautiful women. Praise and thank the creator for the magnificence around you. Wanting to possess it momentarily is selfishness. And it is just finished. When you are able to praise God for the awesome creation, the joy lasts for a long time.

"Be filled with the Spirit, addressing one another in psalms and hymns and spiritual songs, singing and praising the Lord in your hearts, giving thanks always and for everything in the name of our Lord Jesus Christ to God the Father." Ephesians 5:18-20

"You were born an infinite being with unlimited potential, and you still are that magnificence." – Gail Lynne Goodwin

Themes: Hymns, Songs, Choir, Singing, Prayers, Praise, Beauty, Creator, Magnificence, Fundraising, Money, Pastor, Campaign.

91. GRIZZLY BEAR CHASE

Two men were walking through the woods one-day when a large grizzly bear started chasing them. One of the fellows reached into his backpack to retrieve his tennis shoes to change into his heavy hiking boots. His buddy said, "are you crazy? You cannot outrun that bear." The first guy says, "I only have to outrun you."

* * *

Man's worst enemies are not natural catastrophies like earthquake, hurricane, fire, etc. but fellow human beings themselves. We are our own worst enemies. Sometimes we need someone to simply be there ... not to fix anything or do anything in particular, but just to let us feel we are supported and cared for.

Surround yourself with the dreamers and the doers, the believers and thinkers. But most of all surround yourself with those who see greatness within you.

Competitions are not often to bring the best in us but to show that we are better than others. Competition makes us faster; collaboration makes us better. If we win at the expense of others, it is not true victory. True joy comes when we can all be winners.

"I have found the paradox, that if you love until it hurts, there can be no more hurt, only more love." – Mother Teresa

"I accept my uniqueness. There is no competition and no comparison, for we are all different and meant to be that way. I am special and wonderful. I love myself." - Louis L. Hay

Themes: Competition, Friends, Outrun, Love, Sacrifice, Support, Enemies, Men, Buddy, Friends.

92. CONQUERING THE UNIVERSE

A Russian, an American, and a blonde were talking one day. The Russian said, "We were the first in space!"

The American said, "We were the first on the moon!"

The Blonde said, "So what? We're going to be the first on the sun!"

The Russian and the American looked at each other and shook their heads.

"You can't land on the sun, you idiot! You'll burn up!" said the Russian.

To which the Blonde replied, "We're not stupid, you know. We're going at night!"

* * *

The universe is filled with light and darkness and the Creator has His own purpose in designing these energies.

Are you a light-filled or dark-filled person? Positive or Negative? What do you exude most? Good or evil?

People try to do evil in the dark not to be seen by others. But things hidden come to light pretty fast.

"Whatever you have said in the dark will be heard in the light, and what you have whispered behind closed doors will be proclaimed from the housetops." – Luke 12:3

"Every act of evil unleashes a million acts of kindness. This is why shadows will never win while there is still light to shine." – Aaron Paquette

"The world will not be destroyed by those who do evil, but by those who watch them without doing anything." – Albert Einstein

Themes: Negativity, Positivity, Light, Darkness, Good, Evil, Moon, Sun, Blonde, Universe.

93. PASTOR VISITS PARISHIONERS

A new pastor was visiting the homes of his parishioners. At one house, it seemed obvious that someone was at home, but no answer came in spite of his repeated knocks on the door.

Therefore, he took out a business card and wrote, "Revelation 3:20" on the back of it and stuck it in the door.

When the offering was processed the following Sunday, he found that his card had been returned. Added to it was this cryptic message, "Genesis 3:10." Reaching for his Bible to check out the citation, he broke up in gales of laughter.

Revelation 3:20 begins, "Behold, I stand at the door and knock."

Genesis 3:10 reads, "I heard your voice in the garden and I was afraid for I was naked."

* * *

"Ask and it will be given to you; seek and you will find; knock and the door will be opened to you." – Matthew 7:7

Jesus is knocking at the doors of your heart. He will not force his way in. You have to open the doors of your heart from within and allow Him in. Then he can transform your life forever.

Take time to visit a neighbor, a relative, and an old friend. If you do so not only they will be uplifted but you as well. It is in giving that we receive.

A personal open door policy will help openness and transparency. It will help to foster an environment of collaboration, high performance and mutual respect in work places. The mind is like a parachute. It doesn't work unless it's open.

"Honesty and openness is always the foundation of insightful dialogue." – Bell Hooks

"Through the trials and tribulations of life come the openness to receive greatness." – Michelle Cruz Rosado

Themes: Knocking, Expectation, Open Door Policy, Pastor, Parishioners, Visit, Jesus, Neighbor.

94. GIFT OF A CELL PHONE

A young man wanted to get his beautiful blonde wife, Laura, something for their first wedding anniversary. So he decided to buy her a cell phone. He showed her the phone and explained to her all of its features. Laura was excited to receive the gift and simply adored her new phone.

The next day Laura went shopping. Her phone rang and, to her astonishment, it was her husband on the other end.

"Hi, Laura", he said, "how do you like your new phone?"

Laura replied, "I just love it! It's so small and your voice is clear as a bell, but there's one thing I don't understand though"!

What's that, sweetie?" asked her husband.

"How did you know I was at Wal-Mart?"

* * *

Communication helps to pass on vital information, thoughts, and messages. Thanks to the technology, communication today is fast and easier than ever.

Without communication, there is no relationship. If you listen, you may learn something new. Listening is a very vital aspect of good interaction.

You talk because you have a thought, idea or feeling that you want to share with one or more persons. For effective communication, active listening is very important.

"We have but two ears and one mouth so that we may listen twice as much as we speak." – Thomas Edison

"Listen with ears of tolerance. See through the eyes of compassion. Speak with the language of love." – Rumi

Themes: Location, Communication, Listening, Cell Phone, Wife, Husband, Shopping, Anniversary.

95. MISTAKEN OBITUARY

Gallagher opened the morning newspaper and was dumbfounded to read in the obituary column that he had died.

He quickly phoned his best friend Finney. "Did you see the paper?" asked Gallagher. "They say I died!!"

"Yes, I saw it!" replied Finney. "Where are you calling from?"

* * *

Christian, Islamic, Jewish and Zoroastrian religions believe that the dead will be brought back to life. The Bible tells us that when Jesus returns, he will raise all those who have died, giving them back the bodies they lost at death.

The *Catechism of the Catholic Church* states: "We believe in the resurrection from this flesh that we now possess." From the beginning, Christians have prayed for the dead and have undertaken works of penance on their behalf. There is scriptural basis for this intercessory prayer for the sins of others and for the dead in the Old Testament. Job's sacrifices purified his sons (Job 1:5); and Judas Maccabeus "made atonement for the dead that they be delivered from their sin" (II Maccabees 12:46).

Rooted in ancient Christian tradition, St. Odilo of Cluny established a memorial of all the faithful departed in 988. It was accepted in Rome in the 13th century.

The month of November, especially All Souls' Day, is a time for visiting graves of the loved ones, as is the anniversary of death.

"So also is the resurrection of the dead. It is sown corruptible; it is raised incorruptible." – 1 Corinthians 15:42

"We believe that there will be a resurrection of bodies after the consummation of all things." – Tatian the Syrian

Themes: Death, Dead, Obituary, Friend, Call, Heaven, Hell, Religions, Catechism, Catholic, Christians, Prayer, Resurrection, Body.

96. FORGIVE US OUR TRASH PASSES

A 6-year-old was overheard reciting the Lord's Prayer at a church service: "And forgive us our trash passes, as we forgive those who passed trash against us."

* * *

For those who brood over injuries, it may be easier for them to learn Chinese than to say "I'm sorry" or "I forgive you" in our own language.

Forgiveness can be a difficult business. It is often easy for me to love the whole world, but hard to forgive the person who lives or works next to me.

It is said that "to err is human but to forgive is divine". In forgiving, we choose to break the cycle of violence; we refuse to seek revenge for a wrong done. It is not easy. None of us has been perfect in the art of forgiving, but hopefully we have all experienced the freedom that comes with letting go of our hatred. Forgiveness sets us free.

"We have to remember, when we forgive we're not doing it just for the other person, we're doing it for our own good. When we hold on to unforgiveness and we live with grudges in our hearts, all we're doing is building walls of separation." – Joel Osteen

"There is no love without forgiveness and there is no forgiveness without love." – Bryant H. McGill

Themes: Forgiveness, Freedom, Lord's Prayer, Pardon, Mercy, Absolution.

97. An Exit Strategy

A little girl became restless as the preacher's sermon dragged on and on. Finally, she leaned over to her mother and whispered, "Mommy, if we give him the money now, will he let us go?"

* * *

Dream what you want to dream. Go where you want to go. Be what you want to be, because you have only one life and one chance to do all the things you want to do.

No one controls you but yourself. The size of your world is the size of your heart. No matter how hard the past, you can always begin again today.

"Ambition is the germ from which all growth of nobleness proceeds."

– Oscar Wilde

"Freedom means that no one can stop you from doing what

is right, or persuade you to do what is wrong." – Dadi Janki

Themes: Freedom, Dream, Ambition, Life, Sermon, Homily, Message, Pastor, Money, Ambition, Charity, Little Girl.

98. COMMITTAL SERVICE

Little Nancy was in the garden filling in a hole when her neighbor peered over the fence. Interested in what the cheeky-faced youngster was doing, he politely asked, "What are you up to there, Nancy?"

"My bird died," replied Nancy tearfully, without looking up, "and I've just buried him."

The neighbor was concerned, "That's an awfully big hole for a bird, isn't it?"

Nancy patted down the last heap of earth and then replied, "That's because he's inside your cat!"

* * *

The truth is often hidden inside. Often people use certain amount of cover, when they do not want to tell the truth. But the truth finally comes out. So is it not better to tell the truth and be straightforward.

An honest person is always appreciated by everyone around. Truthfulness also gives us peace of mind.

If everyone is truthful and honest, we will not need so many surveillance cameras and guards in public stores. For some dishonesty is bad only if they are caught.

Strive to become more and more honest in words and deeds and we will be happier for that.

If you tell the truth, you don't have to remember anything." – Mark Twain

"Telling the truth and making someone cry is better than telling a lie and making someone smile." – Paolo Coelho

Themes: Honesty, Truth, Genuineness, Lying, Funeral, Neighbor, Cat, Bird.

99. NO MALE PALLBEARERS

An elderly woman died last month. Having never married, she requested no male pallbearers.

In her handwritten instructions for her memorial service, she wrote, "They wouldn't take me out while I was alive, I don't want them to take me out when I'm dead."

* * *

The brightest future will always be based on a forgotten past, you can't go on well in life until you let go of your past failures and heartaches.

Letting go of the past is very difficult for a lot of people. We have to consciously take off the baggage of the past that we carry. Then we can be open to the numerous opportunities of the present and create an amazing future.

"The truth is, unless you let go, unless you forgive yourself, unless you forgive the situation, unless you realize that the situation is over, you cannot move forward." – Steve Maraboli

"Forgetting what lies behind but straining forward to what lies ahead, I continue my pursuit toward the goal, the prize of God's upward calling, in Christ Jesus." – Philippians 3: 13-14

Themes: Future, Failures, Past life, Let Go, Life, Pallbearers, Marriage, Loneliness.

100. CREATION OF HUMAN BEINGS

At Sunday school they were teaching how God created everything, including human beings. Little Johnny seemed especially intent when they told him how Eve was created out of one of Adam's ribs.

Later in the week his mother noticed him lying down as though he were ill, and said, "Johnny, what is the matter?"

Little Johnny responded, "I have pain in my side. I think I'm going to have a wife."

* * *

Family is the nucleus of society. If we have good families, we will have a good society. It is in the family that life begins and love should never end. The family is like branches on a tree, you all grow in different directions yet your roots should remain as one.

Some call matrimony *monotony* because you have one spouse. But if the spouses work together, marriage and family can be delightful.

If marriage has to be bliss, it entails good will and sacrifice from the part of the spouses. Both must be willing to share their joys and sorrows. Every day spend some time in communicating with each other. Both must genuinely care for each other. Show that you care for your spouse very tangibly. It is not enough to love but the other must know that you really love him or her. There will be quarrels and misunderstanding. Be fair to each other and settle disputes fairly.

"For this reason a man will leave his father and mother and be united to his wife, and then they will become one flesh." – Genesis 2:24

"What can you do to promote world peace? Go home and love your family." – Blessed Mother Teresa

Themes: Matrimony, Family, Marriage, Husband, Wife, Monotony, Adam, Eve,

101. DEMANDS OF BEING A CHRISTIAN

After the christening of his baby brother in church, little Johnny sobbed all the way home in the back seat of the car.

His father asked him three times what was wrong. Finally, the boy replied, "That priest said he wanted us brought up in a Christian home, and I want to stay with you guys!"

* * *

A Christian home is where there is the presence of Christ. The family members live the Gospel ideals in the daily lives. The Word of God is translated into action. There is genuine love and respect for one another.

Children will honor their parents and parents will ensure the proper upbringing of the children instilling in them the values and principles of Christ.

Every family should spend a few minutes in praying daily. The family that prays together stays together.

The parents should be role models for the children through an exemplary life. Walk the talk. Examples will be more powerful than words.

"A happy family is but an earlier heaven." – George Bernard Shaw

"You don't choose your family. They are God's gift to you, as you are to them." – Desmond Tutu

Themes: Christian home, Family, Society, Baptism, Christening, Brother, Father, Priest, Presence of Christ, Prayer.

102. PARENTS ARE GREAT

Three boys are in the schoolyard bragging about their fathers.

The first boy says, "My Dad scribbles a few words on a piece of paper, he calls it a poem, they give him $50."

The second boy says, "That's nothing. My Dad scribbles a few words on a piece of paper, he calls it a song, they give him $100."

The third boy says, "I got you both beat. My Dad scribbles a few words on a piece of paper, he calls it a sermon. And it takes eight people to collect all the money!"

* * *

The succinct messages take more time to think out. People who give lengthy sermons, lectures and talks may not be well prepared.

When the speakers love the assembly, they will put themselves in the shoes of the listeners.

Always put yourself in others' shoes. If you feel that it hurts you, it probably hurts the other person too.

"Draw near to God and He will draw near to you." – James 4:8

"I don't know what my future holds, but I do know who holds my future."

– Tim Tebow

Themes: Sermon, Homily, Messages, Speakers, Lectures, Talks, Money, Father, Dad, Usher, Pastor.

103. I Want to Be A Minister

After a church service on Sunday morning, a young boy suddenly announced to his mother, "Mom, I've decided to become a minister when I grow up."

"That's okay with us, but what made you decide that?"

"Well," said the little boy, "I have to go to church on Sunday anyway, and I figure it will be more fun to stand up and yell, than to sit and listen."

* * *

Listening is harder than speaking. We have one mouth and two ears, meaning we are to listen more than talking.

In order to understand the other you have to be an active listener. Listen not only to the verbal message but also to the body language. Be open to the other and do not make judgments.

When you listen to others, you are giving your time, attention and energy. You are recognizing that person as someone important to you. You will have done much good to that person by your patient listening.

"Listening to others viewpoints may reveal the one thing needed to complete your goals." – D. Ridgley

"Trees are the earth's endless effort to speak to the listening heave." – Rabindranath Tagore

Themes: Sermon, Homily, Communication, Listening, Vocation, Attention, Sunday, Minister, Pastor, Priest.

104. GRACE BEFORE MEALS

The Sunday School Teacher asks, "Now, Johnny, tell me frankly do you say prayers before eating?"

"No sir," little Johnny replies, "I don't have to. My mom is a good cook."

* * *

Children do trust their parents. It is the adults who find it difficult to trust one another. You cannot have meaningful relationship without trust. The only way to love and happiness in life is by trusting others. Trust will bring you more friends. To be trusted is a greater compliment than being loved.

It is so very easy to break trust. Trust once lost is hard to regain. Trust takes years to build.

"A man who trusts nobody is apt to be the kind of man nobody trusts." – Harold Macmillan

"Trust is the glue of life. It's the most essential ingredient in effective communication. It's the foundational principle that holds all relationships." – Stephen R. Covey

Themes: Grace, Grace before Meal, Cook, Children, Trust, Prayers, Betrayal, Mom, Mother's Day.

105. PEACE AND CONFLICT

Announcement in the church bulletin: "The peacemaking meeting scheduled for today has been canceled due to a conflict."

* * *

The root of terrorism is misunderstanding, hatred, and violence.

Individuals and nations have to win over their enemies with love. We seek justice and not revenge. Finally, let us remember the words of the Gospel when Jesus asked us to pray for our enemies and to love those who persecute us.

Work for a civilization of love in which there is no room for hatred, discrimination or violence. For true peace, forgiveness is needed.

"Peace cannot be kept by force; it can only be achieved by understanding." – Albert Einstein

"An eye for eye only ends up making the whole world blind" – Mahatma Gandhi

Themes: Peace, Conflict, Hatred, Discrimination, Violence, Forgiveness, Love.

106. TRYING NOT TO BE LATE

A little girl, dressed in her Sunday best, was running as fast as she could, trying not to be late for Bible class. As she ran she prayed, "Dear Lord, please don't let me be late! Dear Lord, please don't let me be late!"

While she was running and praying, she tripped on a curb and fell, getting her clothes dirty and tearing her dress. She got up, brushed herself off, and started running again.

As she ran she once again began to pray, "Dear Lord, please don't let me be late ... but please don't shove me either!"

* * *

Prayer alone is not enough. Prayer and action go together. Your prayers should lead you to action. Find a blend of both. St. James says "prayer without works is dead" – James 2:14-26.

Actions speak louder than words.

The first step is the hardest. Once you begin, the momentum will build and you will progress. Take that action today and do not procrastinate.

"Action is the foundational key to all success." – Pablo Picasso

"Even if you are on the right track, you'll get run over if you just sit there." – Will Rogers

"You may never know what results come from your action. But if you do nothing, there will be no result." – Mahatma Gandhi

Themes: Prayer, Action, Good works, Little Girl, Sunday, Bible Class.

107. PRAYER AND FASTING

Announcement in a church bulletin for a national PRAYER and FASTING Conference: "The cost for attending the Fasting and Prayer conference includes meals."

* * *

Scripture teaches us that fasting and abstaining from food helps us have mastery of the flesh.

It is said that Mahatma Gandhi fasted one day a week. There is growing belief among scientists that fasting can improve long-term health, and reducing food intake over months or year could boost lifespan by 15% to 30%.

Fasting promotes detoxification, rests digestive system, reduces blood sugar, increases fat breakdown and promotes weight loss.

"Fast from anger and hatred; feast on love.

Fast from judging others; feast on openness.

Fast from discouragement; feast on encouragement.

Fast from complaining; feast on appreciating.

Fast from resentment or bitterness; feast on pleasantness.

Fast from spending too much money; feast on charity." – Anonymous

"Fasting is abstaining from anything that hinders prayer." – Andrew Bonar

"Fasting is the greatest remedy – the physician within." – Philippus Paracelsus

Themes: Fast, Lent, Abstention, Penance, Prayer, Conference, Meals, Anger, Hatred, Love, Openness, Charity.

108. HOW TO TREAT OTHERS?

A Sunday school teacher was discussing the Ten Commandments with her five and six year olds. After explaining the commandment to "honor thy father and thy mother," she asked, "Is there a commandment that teaches us how to treat our brothers and sisters?"

Without missing a beat one little boy answered, "Thou shalt not kill."

* * *

When you love and respect others they will also love and respect you. This world is like a cave. When you say, 'good', it echoes back, 'good'. And when you say, 'bad', it echoes back, 'bad'. So also the world around you will reverberate just the way you are.

Always remember the Golden Rule: "Do unto others what you would like them to do to you." Treat others the way you want to be treated. Talk to people the way you want to be talked to. Respect is earned not given.

"We have committed the Golden Rule to memory; let us now commit it to life." – Edwin Markham

"I've learned that people will forget what you said, people will forget what you did, but people will never forget how you made them feel." – Maya Angelou

Themes: Commandment, Relationship, Love, Service, Golden Rule, Treatment, Feeling.

109. NAME DENOMINATION

A blonde woman goes to the post office to buy stamps for her Christmas cards. She says to the clerk, "May I have 50 Christmas stamps?"

The clerk says, "What denomination?"

The woman says, "God help us. Has it come to this? Give me 6 Catholic, 12 Presbyterian, 10 Lutheran and 22 Baptists.

* * *

It is said that "one plus one is three" because of synergy. Unity is strength. Strive to bring about unity and not division. Teamwork and collaboration will bring about success. Your family doesn't have to be perfect; it has to be united.

Unity is not uniformity. It doesn't mean that all of you have to be the same. You have to seek unity in diversity.

All religions speak of love and unity and yet why are there so many divisions and denominations? It is because people are not ready to practice what they preach.

"Even if a unity of faith is not possible, a unity of love is." – Han Urs von Balthasar

"Church unity is like peace, we are all for it, but we are not willing to pay the price." -Dr Visser 't Hooft

Themes: Denominations, Ecumenism, Unity, Division, Peace, Church, Catholic, Presbyterian, Lutheran, Baptists.

110. THE UNSATISFIED GRANMA

There was a grandmother who was walking with her young grandson along a beach. Then a huge wave appeared out of nowhere, sweeping the child out to sea. The horrified woman fell to her knees, raised her eyes to heaven, begged the Lord to return her beloved grandson.

And, lo, another wave reared up and deposited the stunned child on the sand right in front of her. The grandmother looked the boy over carefully. He was fine. But then she stared up angrily toward the heavens. "When we came," she snapped indignantly, "he had a hat! Where is the hat?"

* * *

Somehow we often find it difficult to praise either God or other people. Praise presupposes two elements – the recognition of good in whatever form it comes, and the due acknowledgement of that good through some gesture or action. And we should realize that gratitude isn't only the greatest of attributes, but the parent of them all.

You have 1,440 minutes in a day. How would your life be different if you spent just 15 of those minutes daily giving thanks? Just 15 minutes filling your mind with concrete examples of how fortunate you are? Most of us would discover even after a few days that the exercise was life changing!

"Whether one believes in a religion or not, and whether one believes in rebirth or not, there isn't anyone who doesn't appreciate kindness and compassion." – Dalai Lama

"Appreciation is a wonderful thing: it makes what is excellent in others belong to us as well." – Voltaire

Themes: Appreciation, Thankfulness, Praise, Gratitude, Prayer, Compliment, Tribute, Grandmother, Grandma, Grandson.

111. Sunday Wake Up Call

What happens when the pastor's mom lives in the rectory as his housekeeper? On a Sunday morning he couldn't get out of bed. His mother tried to get him out of bed, but to little avail.

She shouted up the stairs, "Get up!" and he shouted down the stairs, "No!"

Then she shouted again, "Get up!" and he shouted down, "Why should I?"

She said, "Well, first of all your breakfast is ready, secondly this is the third Advent Sunday, and thirdly you're the Pastor and you have to celebrate two Masses".

* * *

You have heard the saying: *Early to bed, early to rise makes a man healthy, wealthy and wise.* If you wake up early, you will be able to accomplish more during the day. Live a disciplined life.

If you are self-disciplined and put on the right thinking cap, you can achieve anything you desire. All successful people are persons of great discipline.

"It is well to be up before daybreak, for such habits contribute to health, wealth, and wisdom." – Aristotle

"Respect your efforts, respect yourself. Self-respect leads to self-discipline. When you have both firmly under your belt, that's real power." – Clint Eastwood

Themes: Pastor, Priest, Church, Parish, Mom, Discipline, Mass, Service, Housekeeper, Rise, Get up, Duty, Responsibility, Sleep, Rest.

112. NEW YEAR'S RESOLUTION

Last year when I called my parents to wish them a Happy New Year, my dad answered the phone. "Well, Dad, what's your New Year's resolution?" I asked him. "To make your mother as happy as I can all year," he answered proudly. Then mom got on, and I said, "What's your resolution, Mom?" "To see that your dad keeps his New Year's resolution."

* * *

It is not your job to ensure that others keep their resolutions. However, the resolutions that you make are indeed very good but you need to keep them. Someone once said: "I made 6 resolutions last year and I kept them all year long: they are in an envelope on the top of my file cabinet."

Devote yourself to your resolution. Be determined to make it happen. Remember that it is your dream.

"How few there are who have courage enough to own their faults, or resolution enough to mend them." - Benjamin Franklin

"When you want to succeed as bad as you want to breathe then you will be successful." – Eric Thomas

Themes: Resolution, Goals, Determination, Perseverance, New Year, Father, Mother.

113. FUN IN THE CHURCH

A man was doing some work in the ceiling of a church. Then an elderly lady came and knelt down before the statue of Mary and started to pray.

The workman decided to have some fun, so he hid himself over the scaffolding and said: "Woman, speak to me. I am Jesus."

The woman did not care but continued to pray to Mary. So the worker repeated again: "Woman, speak to me. I am Jesus."

Then the woman said: "You shut up, I'm talking to your mother."

* * *

Mary the mother of Jesus is the mother of God, since Jesus is God. She is not worshiped but honored. She is the heavenly mother of all people.

With foster-father Joseph, Mary succeeded in training the Child Jesus, so that He grew in holiness and in "favor before God and man." We will honor our heavenly mother if we practice her virtues of faith, obedience, purity and humble service.

"Let us run to Mary and as her little children cast ourselves into her arms with perfect confidence." - St Francis De Sales

"Love our Lady. And she will obtain abundant grace to help you conquer in your daily struggle." – St. Josemaria Escriva

Themes: Mary, Mother, Mother of God, Prayer, Jesus, Prayer, Communication.

114. THE VISION OF THE HOLY FAMILY

A Jesuit, a Dominican and a Franciscan were walking along an old road, debating the greatness of their orders. Suddenly, a vision of the Holy Family appeared in front of them, with Jesus in a manger and Mary and Joseph praying over him.

The Franciscan fell on his face, overcome with awe at the sight of God born in such poverty.

The Dominican fell to his knees, adoring the beautiful reflection of the Trinity and the Holy Family.

The Jesuit walked up to Joseph, put his arm around his shoulder, and said, "So, where are you thinking of sending the kid to school?"

* * *

You call that family of Nazareth a *holy family* because Jesus was the center of Mary and Joseph. When Jesus becomes the center of your family, your family will be holy also. Spend some time daily praying together and reading the Bible. Go as a family to church every weekend.

Every parent has the responsibility to bring up his or her children in the ways of God. You have to educate your children to be good and honest citizens and to have personal relationship with God.

"To overcome today's individualistic mentality, a concrete commitment to solidarity and charity is needed, beginning in the family." – Pope St. John Paul II

"…The peoples of the earth…are called to build relationships of solidarity and cooperation among themselves, as befits members of the one human family." – Pope Benedict XVI

Themes: Jesuit, Dominican, Franciscan, Holy Family, Jesus, Mary, Joseph, Poverty, Trinity, School, Kid, Education.

115. I am John the Baptist

A man who thought he was John the Baptist was disturbing the neighborhood, so for public safety, he was committed. He was put in a room with another crazy one. The new inmate immediately began his routine, "I am John the Baptist! Jesus Christ has sent me!" The other guy looked at him and declared, "I did not!"

* * *

It is important to know oneself. Philosophers of old often said: "Know thyself." So ask yourself: "Who am I?" You have come to know your personality, your core values, your body, your thoughts and your likes and dislikes.

It is not enough to know yourself, what you like, and what you want in life. You have to accept yourself and be happy with yourself. There are people who do hero worship. They try to imitate their heroes in the best way possible. Live your life and not someone else's.

"Be yourself; everyone is already taken." - Aristotle

"Knowing others is intelligence, knowing yourself is true wisdom." – Lao Tzu

Themes: John the Baptist, Jesus Christ, Craze, Pretend, Genuineness, Truth, Honesty, Life, Self-Image, Self-acceptance.

116. ANNIVERSARY GIFT

With a couple celebrating their 50th anniversary at the church's marriage marathon, the minister asked Ralph to take a few minutes and share some insight into how he managed to live with the same woman all these years.

The husband replied to the audience, "Well, I treated her with respect, spent money on her, but mostly I took her out and travelled on special occasions."

The minister inquired trips to where?

"For our 25th anniversary, I took her to Beijing, China."

The minister then said, "What a terrific example you are to all husbands, Ralph. Please tell the audience what you're going to do for your wife on your 50th anniversary?"

Ralph: "I'm going to go get her."

* * *

Jubilees and anniversaries are a time to look back and give thanks to God for His manifold blessings. Every moment that you have is a gift from God that is freely given. It is God who brought you together in a family. Make Him the center of your family. "The family that prays together stays together."

Jesus says: "Love one another as I have loved you." (John 15:12) Couples often choose this Gospel to read at their wedding ceremony. How has Jesus loved you? He loved you to the extent that He gave his life for you. In order to make the marriage successful, couples have to give to each other sacrificially.

"Let them thank the Lord for his mercy, such wondrous deeds for the children of Adam. For he satisfied the thirsty filled the hungry with good things." – Psalm 107: 8-9

"You will reciprocally promise love, loyalty and matrimonial honesty. We only want for you this day that these words constitute the principle of your entire life and that with the help of divine grace you will observe these solemn vows that today, before God, you formulate." - St. Pope John Paul II

Themes: Jubilee, Anniversary, Wedding, Marriage, Gift, Husband, Wife, Minister, Priest, Unity, Family.

117. COLOR OF HAPPINESS

Attending a wedding for the first time, a little girl whispered to her mother, "Why is the bride dressed in white?"

"Because white is the color of happiness, and today is the happiest day of her life."

The child thought about this for a moment, then said, "So why is the groom wearing black?"

* * *

Don't go for looks; they can deceive. Don't go for wealth; even that fades away. Go for someone who makes you smile because it takes only a smile to make a dark day seem bright.

Find the one that makes your heart smile.

Look for a heart that is warm and caring not for skin beauty that will disappear. Look for a soul that is self-confident and giving and not for bodily shape that is pleasing to the eye. Life's most beautiful things are not seen with the eyes but felt with the heart.

Happiest people don't have the best of everything; they just make the best of everything.

"You aren't wealthy until you have something money can't buy." --Garth Brooks

"Love is your true destiny. We do not find the meaning of life by ourselves alone – we find it with another." – Thomas Merton

Themes: Wedding, Marriage, Smile, Appearance, Happiness, Family, Mother,

118. WANTS A RIDE HOME

The man dropped off his wife at the hairstylist and she was supposed to call him when she was ready to be picked up. She must have dialed a wrong number. She called, and a man said, "Hello," to which she cheerfully said, "come and get me!"

The man said, "Are you sure? This is Mitchell's funeral home."

* * *

People want to go to heaven, but no one wants to die to get there. The mystery of death is cruel, final, irrevocable, absurd, and vicious. It can make everything that goes before in life appear a sham.

We live in a world of paradox. There is so much wonder in it, so much splendor in it, so much fun and amusement. On the other hand, one is faced with the violence, suffering, injustice, and death. How can all this suffering, all this agony, all this darkness be reconciled with the God who claims he is a God of love, of mercy and of tenderness?

It is in the resurrection of Christ and his promise of resurrection for us that this problem is resolved. We look at death as a passage from this life to next life, then we can begin to see the face of God even behind everything that crushes our life. The hope of resurrection changes all the equations.

"Death is the golden key that opens the palace of eternity." – John Milton

"Every deceased friend is a magnet drawing us into another world." – Eliza Cook

Themes: Funeral, Funeral Home, Mortuary, Death, Heaven, End Times, Bereavement, Mortality, Decease, Communication.

119. Choosing a Profession

There was an old country preacher who had a teenage son, and it was getting time that the boy should give some thought along the line of choosing a profession.

Like many young men, then and now, the boy didn't really know what he wanted to do and he didn't seem overly concerned about it.

One day, while the boy was away at school, his father decided to try an experiment.

What he did was to go into the boy's room and place on his study table these three objects: a Bible, a silver dollar, and a bottle of whiskey.

"Now then," the old preacher said to himself, "I'll just hide behind the door here, and when my son comes home from school this afternoon, I'll see which of these three objects he picks up.

If he picks up the Bible, he's going to be a preacher like me, and what a blessing that would be!

If he picks up the dollar, he's going to be a businessman, and that would be o.k. too.

But if he picks up the bottle, he's going to be a drunkard - a no-good drunkard, and Lord, what a shame that would be!"

The old man was anxious as he waited, and soon he heard his son's footsteps as he came in the house whistling and headed back to his room.

He deposited his books on the bed, as a matter of routine, and as he turned around to leave the room he spotted the objects on the table.

With a curious set in his eye, he walked over to inspect them.

What he finally did was, he picked up the Bible and placed it under his arm.

He picked up the silver dollar and dropped it into his pocket.

He uncorked the bottle and took a big drink.

"Lord have mercy," the old man whispered, "He's going to be a politician!"

* * *

Every profession is noble. Look at your vocation as a spiritual calling. What is important is to love and enjoy what you do. Then your profession will not be a tedious work for you.

Never be afraid to try something new. Remember, an amateur built the ark; professionals built the Titanic. Experiment withsomething new and that will help you to be creative and may lead to making inventions.

"I think it's imperative to follow your heart and choose a profession you're passionate about, and if you haven't found that 'spark' yet, if you're not sure what you want to do with your lives – be persistent until you do." – Steve Kerr

"I stretch myself to new levels of excellence every day. I choose to be better this very moment." – Nadeem Kazi

Themes: Bible, Alcohol, Whiskey, Money, Dollar, Politician, Vocation, Profession, Creativity, Invention.

120. DIVORCE SETTLEMENT

"Mr. Clark, I have reviewed this case very carefully," the divorce Court Judge said, "And I've decided to give your wife $775 a week."

That's very fair, your honor," the husband said. "And every now and then I'll try to send her a few bucks myself."

* * *

The family that prays together stays together. Prayer and worship can be linked to better health, longer marriages and better family life.

Divorce is often a painful process for both the parties. As the couples are emotionally torn apart the children too are dragged along. The divorce of parents, even if it is amicable, tears apart the fundamental unit of the society.

There are times when you have to let go. You don't want to remain in unhappy relationship forever. Be with someone who brings the best in you, not the stress in you.

"You may not control all the events that happen to you, but you can decide not to be reduced by them." – Maya Angelou

"New beginnings are often disguised as painful endings." - Lao Tzu

Themes: Marriage, Divorce, Judge, Wedding, Husband, Wife.

121. DON'T LIKE THE LOOKS

A doctor examined a woman, took the husband aside, and said, "I don't like the looks of your wife at all."

"Me neither Doc," said the husband. "But she's a great cook and really good with the kid."

* * *

The impression given by one's physical appearance could be totally different to that person's character. There are people who hide their real character and show a different personality. Judging a person by his or her appearance will be misleading, irrational and could be unfair.

Sometimes those who appear nice are ugly and those who appear ugly are nice.

Genuine love doesn't care about body type, model looks, or wallet size. It only cares about what's inside the person. A beautiful personality will last a lifetime while the appearance will last only for a few decades.

"Stop judging and you will not be judged. Stop condemning and you will not be condemned. Forgive and you will be forgiven." Luke 6:37

"Appearance is something absolute, but reality is not that way – everything is interdependent, not absolute." – Dalai Lama

Themes: External Appearance, Looks, Judgment, First Impressions, Doctor, Husband, Wife, Family.

122. Pastor's Twenty-fifth Anniversary

A parish priest was being honored at a dinner on the twenty-fifth anniversary of his arrival in that parish. A leading local politician, who was a member of the congregation, was chosen to make the presentation and give a little speech at the dinner, but he was delayed in traffic, so the priest decided to say his own few words while they waited.

"You will understand," he said, "the seal of the confessional can never be broken. However, I got my first impressions of the parish from the first confession I heard here. I can only hint vaguely about this, but when I came here twenty-five years ago I thought I had been assigned to a terrible place. The very first chap who entered my confessional told me how he had stolen a television set, and when stopped by the police, had almost murdered the officer. Further, he told me he had embezzled money from his place of business and had an affair with his boss's wife. I was appalled. But as the days went on I knew that my people were not all like that, and I had, indeed, come to a fine parish full of understanding and loving people."

Just as the priest finished his talk, the politician arrived full of apologies at being late. He immediately began to make the presentation and give his talk.

"I'll never forget the first day our parish priest arrived in this parish," said the politician. "In fact, I had the honor of being the first one to go to him for confession."

* * *

Most cultures consider punctuality important. When we are on time, we are strengthening and revealing our integrity. Being on time shows that we keep our word. When we practice punctuality we show that we are dependable. Being punctual builds our self-confidence, reveals our discipline, shows that we respect others.

Being late consistently makes us unreliable. Being tardy is for some people a habit. Remember that every bad habit can be broken.

"Arriving late is a way of saying that your own time is more valuable than the time of the person who waited for you." – Karen Joy Fowler

"I never could have done what I have done without the habits of punctuality, order, and diligence, without the determination to concentrate myself on one subject at a time." – Charles Dickens

Themes: Punctuality, Time, Priest, Parish Priest, Politician, Confession, Reconciliation, Penance, Sin.

123. FLYING TIME

A blonde calls one of the Airlines and asks, "Can you tell me how long it'll take to fly from San Francisco to New York City?"

The agent replies, "Just a minute."

"Thank you," the blonde says, and hangs up.

* * *

It is said that we have two ears and one mouth that we may listen more than we speak. When someone is speaking, most people are already mentally preparing the next thing that they are going to say as soon as the person takes a breath.

When we listen attentively to another, we respect the other and are totally present to that person. Listening skills help us to make sense and understand what another person is saying. Good listening can improve the content and quality of what we hear and remember.

Here are a few good listening tips: maintain eye contact,

don't interrupt the speaker, sit still, nod your head, lean toward the speaker, and ask questions or clarifications.

"The first duty of love is to listen." – Paul Tillich

"Silence is a source of great strength." – Lao Tzu

Themes: Communication, Listening, Speaking, Blonde, Airlines, Time, Flight.

124. REMOVE THE CURSE

An old man goes to the Wizard to ask him if he can remove a curse he has been living with for the last 40 years.

The Wizard says, "Maybe, but you will have to tell me the exact words that were used to put the curse on you".

The old man says without hesitation, "I now pronounce you man and wife."

* * *

Family is the nucleus of society. But today, as increasing divorce rates indicate, families are breaking apart. Many people are not able to appreciate the sanctity of marriage. God wills the union of husband and wife and it symbolizes the marriage of Christ and his Church.

Good communication between husband and wife is necessary for understanding and accepting each other in marriage. Marriage calls for sacrificial, unconditional love for each other. When misunderstandings or fights occur, reconcile and make peace at the earliest.

"Successful marriage requires falling in love many times, always with the same person." – Mignon McLaughlin

"The best part of life is when your family becomes your friends and your friends become your family."

Themes: Marriage, Wedding, Matrimony, Family, Friends, Divorce, Curse, Wife, Husband, Communication, Love, Relationship.

125. REMEDY FOR OVERWEIGHT

A blonde is terribly overweight, so her doctor put her on a diet. "I want you to eat regularly for two days, then skip a day, and repeat this procedure for two weeks. The next time I see you, you'll have lost at least 5 pounds." When the blonde returned, she shocked the doctor by losing 20 pounds.

"Why, that's amazing!" the doctor said, "Did you follow my instructions?"

The blonde nodded, "I'll tell you though, I thought I was going to drop dead that third day."

"From hunger, you mean?" Asked the doctor.

"No, from skipping."

* * *

Obesity is a major health hazard today. Poor eating habits and lack of sufficient physical exercises contribute to it. Lots of people are habituated to eating fast food and drinking sodas which are not very healthy. Some people spend large amount of time before television, becoming couch potatoes. Obesity increases our risk of diseases and health problems such as heart disease, diabetes and high blood pressure.

One can lose weight through dietary changes, increased physical activity and behavior changes. Eating in small portions and quitting with the junk food will help lose weight.

"The way you think, the way you behave, the way you eat, can influence your life by 30 to 50 years." – Deepak Chopra

"A healthy body is a guest-chamber for the soul; a sick body is a prison."

– Francis Bacon

Themes: Over Weight, Obesity, Fat, Dieting, Food, Drink, Exercise, Health, Life.

126. Whose Intelligence?

A little boy went up to his father and asked: "Dad, where did all of my intelligence come from?"

The father replied. "Well son, you must have got it from your mother, because I still have mine."

* * *

Compared to animals, human beings are highly intelligent. We have the ability to learn, reason and solve issues. We can be introspective and that sets us apart from animals.

The real sign of intelligence is imagination. Good imagination can lead you to creativity. Your thoughts become things. What you constantly think will become a reality for you. So you have to choose your thoughts really well.

"Everything in the universe has a purpose. Indeed, the invisible intelligence that flows through everything in a purposeful fashion is also flowing through you." – Wayne Dyer

"There are three main ingredients to success: intelligence, creativity and confidence. If you have those three you can rule the world." -- Olianna Port

Themes: Parents, Family, Intelligence, Father, Mother, Children, Thought, Creativity, Confidence, Boy, Dad.

127. JOIN THE ARMY OF THE LORD

A young man was coming out of church one day, and the pastor was standing at the door as always to shake hands.

The pastor grabbed the young man by the hand and pulled him aside. "Young man," he said to him, "you need to join the Army of the Lord!"

The young man replied, "I'm already in the Army of the Lord, Pastor."

The pastor questioned, "How come I don't see you except at Christmas and Easter?"

He whispered back, "I'm in the Secret Service."

* * *

Some go to church only three times in their lifetime, i.e. when hatched, matched and dispatched. When hatched for baptism, when matched for marriage and when dispatched for funeral.

Frequent participation at Mass or church services helps us to come closer to God and build a relationship with Him. Draw near to God and He will draw near to you (James 4:8). We need the power and presence of God with us to accomplish our mission on earth.

In the Bible we read that Jesus often went to pray. When we spend time in the church in prayer, we will encounter God and we will receive much peace, love and joy. Gradually we will become Christ-like in our attitude and behavior.

"You can be committed to Church but not committed to Christ, but you cannot be committed to Christ and not committed to Church." – Joel Osteen

Just going to Church doesn't make you a Christian any more than standing in your garage makes you a car." – G. K. Chesterton

Themes: Prayer, Mass, Eucharist, Faith, Sunday, Service, Army, Pastor, Church, Greeting.

128. BEGINNING OF HUMAN RACE

A little girl asked her father: "How did the human race first appear?"

The father answered: "God made Adam and Eve and they had children and so was all mankind made."

Two days later the girl asked her mother the same question.

The mother answered: "Many years ago, there were monkeys from which the human race evolved."

The confused girl returned to her father and said: "Dad how is it possible, that you told me the human race was created by God, and Mom said we developed from monkeys?"

The father answered: "Well, dear, it is very simple. I told you about my side of the family and your mother told you about hers."

* * *

Children ask all sorts of questions. We are bombarded with all kinds of questions even from adults such as: "What will you become when you grow up?" Soon they will ask: "Will you ever grow up".

It is important to ask the right questions, to elicit the right answers. Asking the right questions also make one think critically. It is the key to business success and essential for setting effective business strategy.

"There's nothing more dangerous than the right answer to the wrong question." – Peter Drucker

"Quality questions create a quality life. Successful people ask better questions, and as a result, they get better answers." – Anthony Robbins

Themes: Evolution, Creation, Human Race, Questions, Asking Questions, First Parents, Parents, Father, Mother, Girl.

129. ONE FOR YOU AND ONE FOR ME

On the outskirts of town, there was a big old pecan tree by the cemetery fence. One day two boys filled up a bucketful of nuts and sat down by the tree, out of sight, and began dividing the nuts. "One for you, one for me. One for you, one for me," said one boy. Several were dropped and rolled down toward the fence.

Another boy came riding along the road on his bicycle. As he passed, he thought he heard voices from inside the cemetery. He slowed down to investigate. Sure enough, he heard, "One for you, one for me. One for you, one for me." He just knew what it was. "Oh my," he shuddered; it's Satan and the Lord dividing the souls at the cemetery. He jumped back on his bike and rode off. Just around the bend he met an old man with a cane, hobbling along.

"Come here quick," said the boy, "you won't believe what I heard. Satan and the Lord are down at the cemetery dividing up the souls. "The man said, "Beat it kid, can't you see it's hard for me to walk." When the boy insisted, though, the man hobbled to the cemetery. Standing by the fence they heard, "One for you, one for me. One for you, one for me." The old man whispered, "Boy, you've been telling the truth. Let's see if we can see the devil himself."

Shaking with fear, they peered through the fence, yet were still unable to see anything. The old man and the boy gripped the wrought iron bars of the fence tighter and tighter as they tried to get a glimpse of Satan.

At last they heard, "One for you, one for me. And one last one for you. That's all. Now let's go get those nuts by the fence, and we'll be done."

They say the old guy made it back to town five minutes before the boy.

* * *

God wants everyone to be saved. Your destiny is heaven where you will behold the face of God in the presence of angels and saints. Jesus has gone to prepare a place for everyone. He wants you to be there with Him.

Life here on earth is just a preparation for eternity with God. Invest well your time, talents and treasures. Your eternity will depend upon how well you have invested those and how well you have lived.

"Physical beauty is only skin deep but the beauty of the soul is infinite."

– Doe Zantamata

"Happiness resides not in possessions and not in gold, happiness dwells in the soul." – Democritus

Themes: God, Satan, Devil, Cemetery, Soul, Salvation, Heaven, Eternity, Happiness.

130. THE DETERMINED CEO

A company, feeling it was time for a shakeup, hired a new CEO. This new boss was determined to rid the company of all slackers.

On a tour of the facilities, the CEO notices a guy leaning on the wall. The room is full of workers, and he wants to let them know he means business.

The CEO walks up to the guy and asks, "And, how much do YOU make a week?" A little surprised, the young fellow looks at him and replies, I make

$300.00 per week. Why?"

The CEO then hands the guy $600.00 in cash and screams, "Here's two weeks' pay, now get out and don't come back!"

Feeling pretty good about his first firing, the CEO looks around the room and asks, "Does anyone want to tell me what that 'goof-off' did here?"

One of the workers said, "He's a pizza delivery guy from Dominoes!"

* * *

Think before you leap. Think carefully about what you are about to do before you do it. Do not rush into making decisions that will make you regret. Look at issues from different angles before you make conclusions.

Before you make a final decision, really think about what you are doing and ask yourself ... is it worth it?

"I am always wary of decisions made hastily. I am always wary of the first decision, that is, the first thing that comes to my mind if I have to make a decision. This is usually the wrong thing. I have to wait and assess, looking deep into myself, taking necessary time." – Pope Francis

"With or without God, good decisions can be made; but only with God will great decisions be made." – Damon Thueson

Themes: Decision, Decision Making, CEO, Determination, Firing, Business, Boss, Company.

131. BILL OR QUARTERS

A young boy enters a barbershop and the barber whispers to his customer, "This is the dumbest kid in the world. Watch while I prove it to you."

The barber puts a dollar bill in one hand and two quarters

in the other, then calls the boy over and asks, "Which do you want, son?" The boy takes the quarters and leaves.

"What did I tell you?" said the barber. "That kid never learns!"

Later, when the customer leaves, he sees the same young boy coming out of the ice cream store. "Hey, son! May I ask you a question? Why did you take the quarters instead of the dollar bill?"

The boy licked his cone and replied, "Because the day I take the dollar, the game is over".

* * *

Life is faced with choices. The choices you make have consequences. Make wise choices that will give you lasting peace.

What is in your life now is the result of choices you have made. If you need a different result, make a different choice. No matter how far you've gone down the wrong road you can always make a U turn.

"Your life is a result of the choices you make … If you don't like your life it is time to start making better choices." – Anonymous

"Weigh your decision: It is going to bring harm to even one person or build tension in your own mind, it's not a good decision." – Swami Satchidananda

Themes: Choices, Decision, Life, Game, Winner, Dumb, Dollar, Money, Gift.

132. Do Something About the Side Walks

An old priest got sick of everyone in his parish confessing adultery. During one Sunday's sermon he told them, "If one more person confesses to adultery, I'll quit!"

Since everyone liked him, they decided to use a code word: "fallen." From then on, anyone who had committed adultery said they had "fallen." This satisfied the old priest and the parishioners, and everything was fine for years, until finally the old priest passed away at the ripe old age of 93.

Shortly after the new young priest settled in, he paid a call on the mayor. The priest was quite concerned. "You have to do something about the sidewalks in this town, Mayor. You can't believe how many people come into the confessional talking about having fallen!" The mayor started to laugh, realizing that no one had explained their code word to the new priest.

But before the mayor could explain, the priest shook his finger at the mayor and said, "I don't know why you're laughing; your wife fell three times last week!"

* * *

According to the Catechism of the Catholic Church, sin is an offense against reason, truth, right conscience; it is failure in genuine love for God and neighbor caused by perverse attachment to certain good. It wounds the nature of man and injures human solidarity.

Sin is an offense against God and damages your relationship with God. But if you repent and confess your sins, God will forgive you. God wants your transformation. Every sinner has a future.

God is loving and forgiving. If God didn't forgive sinners, heaven would be empty.

"Hate the sin, love the sinner." – Mahatma Gandhi

"Your sin is not greater than God's mercy." – Nouman Ali Khan

Themes: Sin, Confusion, Misunderstanding, Confession, Mercy, Forgiveness, Adultery, Priest, Mayor, Ignorance, Politician.

133. FORGIVE YOUR ENEMIES

Sunday's sermon was "Forgive Your Enemies." Toward the end of the service the minister asked, "How many of you have forgiven your enemies?"

80% held up their hands. The minister then repeated his question. All responded this time except one small, elderly lady.

"Mrs. Jones, are you not willing to forgive your enemies?"

"I don't have any," she replied, smiling sweetly.

"Mrs. Jones, that is very unusual. How old are you?"

"Ninety-eight," she replied.

"Oh Mrs. Jones, would you please come down in front and tell us all how a person can live ninety-eight years and not have an enemy in the world?"

The little sweetheart of a lady tottered down the aisle, faced the congregation and said, "I outlived the bitches."

* * *

If you harbor anger or hatred, you are the one suffering and not the other. Let go off bitterness, resentment, regret and remorse. Don't live in the past, move forward. Look at the big front windshield and don't look at the small rear window all the time.

When negative thoughts come, do not relive them like a movie channel. Quickly take the remote control and change the channel. Let go of your failures and disappointments; you can't do anything about the past, but you can do much about the future.

"Without forgiveness life is governed by an endless cycle of resentment and retaliation." – Roberto Assagioli

"Unforgiveness is choosing to stay trapped in a jail cell of bitterness, serving time for someone else's crime." – Anonymous

Themes: Forgiveness, Pardon, Sermon, Enemies, Minister, Long Life, Bitterness, Resentment, Regret, Remorse.

134. SICK VISIT

When Bishop Philip Brooks, author of "O, Little Town of Bethlehem," was seriously ill, he requested that none of his friends come to see him. But when an acquaintance of his named Robert Ingersoll, the famous anti-Christian propagandist, came to see him he allowed him to enter his room.

Ingersoll said, "I appreciate this very much, especially when you aren't letting any of your close friends see you."

Bishop Brooks responded, "Oh, I'm confident of seeing them in the next world, but this may be my last chance to see you."

* * *

This world is only a passage to eternity with God. Live your life to the full caring and loving all God's creation. The Christian belief is that if you live a good life, your souls will be in heaven forever. You will be reunited with your family and dear ones in the next life.

Live your life as if each day is your last day. Count your blessings and be prepared for your journey to God.

"It gives me a deep comforting sense that things seen are temporal and things unseen are eternal." – Helen Keller

"For small reward a man will hurry away on a long journey, while for eternal life many will hardly take a single step." – Thomas a Kempis

Themes: Eternal Life, Eternity, Salvation, Resurrection, Heaven, Hell, Friends.

135. THE SAD TALE OF A DOLLAR BILL

A one-dollar bill met a 100-dollar bill and said, "Hey, where've you been? I haven't seen you around here much."

The 100 answered, "I've been hanging out at the casinos, went on a cruise and did the rounds of the ship, back to the United States for a while, went to a couple of baseball games, to the mall, that kind of stuff. How about you?"

The one-dollar bill said, "You know, same old stuff, to church, to church, and to church."

* * *

The Biblical norm is to tithe to God. You are invited to offer to God 10% of all that you make. Tithing is not for God; he doesn't need your money. It is for your benefit; to teach you to trust God in many ways. God needs to be first in your life and so give God the first part of your money. It is also a way to show your gratitude to God. Tithing releases joy, prosperity and favor in your life.

As good stewards, you have to offer certain amount of time, talent and treasure to God. Also when you give that to another in need, you are giving to God himself.

"No one has ever become poor by giving." – Anne Frank

"As we give, we find that sacrifice brings forth the blessings of heaven, and in the end, we learn it was no sacrifice at all." – Spencer W. Kimball

Themes: Money, Dollar, Donation, Offering, Giving, Trips, Church, Tithe, Time, Talent, Treasure.

136. REMEMBER YOU ARE DUST

It was Ash Wednesday and the church was packed with people. Matt, the sacristan offered to help. "OK," said Father, "now these are the words you say: 'Remember, man, you are dust, and to dust you shall return."

Matt prepared to start at the back of the church. But Matt came hurrying over to the priest: "Father, what are those words again?" Father told him, Matt went back to his station, but in a moment he was back, asking for the words, which Father repeated.

When Matt came back the third time Father exploded: "You are a dummy and you'll always be a dummy."

Matt didn't come back but when the priest and the sacristan came close to each other at the middle the priest was dumbfounded to hear the words Matt was saying: "You are a dummy and you'll always be a dummy"

* * *

Life is short and so live your life to the fullest. The thought of death is morbid yet one has to think about mortality. On your tombstone your date of birth and death is separated by a little dash. That little dash signifies your time on earth. What is important is how well you live that little dash of time. Live in the light of eternity.

The degree to which you believe in the resurrection of the dead will determine the way that you presently live. If you truly believe in the resurrection, then you will boldly stand for Christ and for your brothers and sisters, not fearing death. If you believe that this world is not the end, you will look at this life very differently. It will totally change your "investment strategy" – of your time, energy and money – your very lives.

"As a well-spent day brings happy sleep, so a life well used brings happy death." – Leonardo da Vinci

"What a caterpillar calls the end of the world the master calls a butterfly." – Richard Bach

Themes: Ash Wednesday, Conversion, Repentance, Lent, Dummy, Resurrection, Death, Dead, Mortality, Eternity.

137. Husband Has A Problem

"I hope you didn't take it personally, Father," an embarrassed woman said to her pastor after the Mass, "that my husband walked out during your homily."

"I did find it rather disconcerting," the preacher replied.

"It's not a reflection on you, Father," she insisted. "Ralph has been walking in his sleep ever since he was a child."

* * *

Public speaking is an art that it is not easy for most people. Every person with determination and practice can do public speaking. Avoid being boring and monotonous. Be well prepared and speak with passion.

It is said that the speech should have a strong start and a great end and the distance between the two must be short. It should be like "KISS", the acronym means, "Keep it short and simple."

"My father gave me these tips on speech making. Be sincere, be brief and be seated." – James Roosevelt

"All the great speakers were bad speakers at first." – Ralph Waldo Emerson

Themes: Sermon, Homily, Message, Public Speaking, Speech, Pastor, Priest, Father, Mass, Sleep.

138. COUNTING THE SHEEP

There was a typical blond. She had long, blond hair, blue eyes, and she was sick of all the blond jokes. One day, she decided to get a makeover, so she cut and dyed her hair. She also went out and bought a new convertible. She went driving down a country road and came across a herd of sheep. She stopped and called the sheepherder over.

"That's a nice flock of sheep," she said.

"Well thank you" said the herder.

"Tell you what. I have a proposition for you" said the woman. "If I can guess the exact number of sheep in your flock, can I take one home?"

"Sure" said the sheepherder.

So, the girl sat up and looked at the herd for a second and then replied "382".

"Wow" said the herder. "That is exactly right. Go ahead and pick out the sheep you want to take home."

So the woman went and picked one out and put it in her car.

Then, the herder said "Okay, now I have a proposition for you".

"What is it?" Queried the woman.

"If I can guess the real color of your hair, can I have my dog back?"

* * *

"I am the good shepherd, and I know mine and mine know me." (John 10:14). God knows you thoroughly. Jesus said even the hair on your head is counted. You are so very precious and important to him.

Do you know Jesus Christ well? To know Him well, you have to spend time in prayer and meditation. You have to study the Scriptures and teachings of the Church. Knowledge of Jesus can help in your relationship with Him.

"Always live under the eyes of the Good Shepherd and you will walk unharmed through evil pastures." – St. Padre Pio

"The love of God is passionate. He pursues each of us even when we know it not." – William Wordsworth

Themes: Good Shepherd, Sheep, Bible Study, God, Jesus Christ, Prayer, Meditation, Scriptures, Church.

139. I DIDN'T DO IT

A Sunday school teacher was telling the students of how the walls of Jericho came down amazingly by the blowing of trumpets and shouts of the people. Observing that Johnny was daydreaming, the teacher asked him: "Johnny who knocked down the walls of Jericho?" Johnny started shouting furiously, "I didn't do it, I didn't do it!," and he ran from the class in protest.

That evening the teacher met his parents in the park and spoke to Johnny's mother. She told her the story of what happened in the class and about Johnny's unreasonable outburst in the class. His mother said, "If my son said he didn't do it, then he didn't do it! I trained him not to tell lies." The perplexed teacher asked Johnny's mother if she could speak to the boy's father.

When she explained the incident to him he said: "Let's not fuss about this. Just tell me how much it will cost to repair the walls and I'll write a check."

* * *

Ignorance is not always bliss. Knowledge is power. Man is a thinking animal. We are born to think, to study, and invent. Knowledge helps us to live a quality life.

We can learn something new every day. Knowledge and information help us solve problems. We have to have the wisdom and knowledge to understand why certain things happen in our lives. Be a lifelong learner.

"Human behavior flows from three main sources: desire, emotion, and knowledge." – Plato

"Today knowledge has power. It controls access to opportunity and advancement." – Peter Drucker

Themes: Knowledge, Ignorance, Irresponsibility, Unawareness, Sunday School, Teacher, Parents, Son, Mother, Father.

140. GO UP OR DOWN

A tour group had ridden elevators to the top of the Empire State Building. At about the 102nd floor, a woman asked the tour guide, "If the cables on this elevator break, do we go up or down?"

The tour guide answered, "Well, that depends on how you have been living."

* * *

Life on earth is short. It is like a blink of eye compared to eternity. Your destiny is heaven. You have only a temporary home here but your permanent home is to be with God in the presence of angels and saints.

You have to live in the light of eternity. All that you do with your time, talent and treasure have to be geared up to reach your final destination, which is heaven.

"Among the many signs of a lively faith and hope we have in eternal life, one of the surest is not being overly sad at the death of those whom we dearly love in our Lord." – Saint Ignatius

"The mind is its own place and in itself, can make a Heaven of Hell, a Hell of Heaven." – John Milton

Themes: Eternity, Eternal Life, Elevator, Heaven, Hell, Life, Living, Goodness.

141. Seat at the Super Bowl

A young man was very excited because he just won a ticket to the Super Bowl. His excitement lessened as he realized his seat was in the back of the stadium. As he searched the rows ahead of him for a better seat, he saw an empty one right next to the field. He approached the man sitting next to the empty seat and asked if it was taken.

The man replied, "No." Amazed the young man asked, "How could someone pass up a seat like this?"

The older gentleman responded, "That's my wife's seat. We've been to every Super Bowl together since the day we were married but she has passed away."

"Oh, how sad," the man said. "I'm sorry to hear that, but couldn't you find a friend or relative to come with you?" "No," the man said, "They're all at the funeral."

* * *

Unconditional love sustains marriage. Both husband and wife ought to ask themselves: "How can I serve my spouse better today?" Good communication is essential for a healthy marriage. Do not just talk about what is going on at the sports arena, political field and weather channel. But every day spend some time talking about your feelings and emotions.

Forgiveness is very important for a happy marriage. Since you are made up of flesh and blood small fights, quarrels, exchange of words could occur. When that happens, reconcile and make peace. Never go to bed angry with your spouse.

"A happy marriage is the union of two good forgivers." – Ruth Bell Graham

"Marriage is a mosaic you build with your spouse. Millions of tiny moments that create your love story." – Jennifer Smith

Themes: Super Bowl, Game, Death, Funeral, Relationship, Husband, Wife, Young Man, Marriage, Family.

142. WHAT GETS ME TO HEAVEN

The Sunday school teacher was testing children in her class to see if they understood the concept of getting to heaven. She asked them, "If I sold my house and my car, had a big jumbo sale and gave all my money to the church, would that get me into heaven?"

"No!" the children answered.

"If I cleaned the church every day, mowed the garden, and kept everything tidy, would that get me into heaven?"

Again, the answer was 'No!'

"Well, then, if I were kind to animals and gave candies to all the children, and loved my husband, would that get me into heaven?"

Again, they all answered 'No!' She continued, "Then how can I get into Heaven?"

A six-year old boy shouted from the back. "First, you have to die!"

* * *

Create heaven on earth by being a good steward. Share generously your time, talent and treasure with your church or a charitable organization that you like. Heaven is not for people who are better than others but for people who earnestly try to become better than they already are.

Everyone wants to go to heaven but no one wants to die. No one can escape death and hence must live in the light of eternity.

"The way you store up treasure in heaven is by investing in getting people there." – Rick Warren

"Go to heaven for the climate, hell for the company." – Mark Twain

Themes: Death, Heaven, Hell, Church, Charity, Stewardship, Children.

143. ADAM'S QUESTIONS

One day, while he was walking with God in the Garden of Eden Adam said, "Excuse me God, can I ask you a few questions?"

God replied, "Go on Adam, but be quick. I have a world to create."

So Adam says, "When you created Eve, why did you make her body so curved and tender unlike mine?"

"I did that, Adam, so that you could love her."

"Oh, well then, why did you give her long, shiny, beautiful hair?"

"I did that Adam so that you could love her."

"Oh, well then, why did you make her so stupid? Is that too because I should love her?"

"Well, Adam, no. I did that so that she could love you."

* * *

To love and to be loved is a need for human beings. But love is often mistaken for sex and lust. Love is a deep, tender, ineffable feeling of affection toward a person.

True love is knowing a person's culpabilities and loving them even more for them. You must try to care for another person's happiness more than your own.

"True love is not so much a matter of romance as it is a matter of anxious concern for the well being of one's companion." – Gordon B. Hinckley

"Love is patient, love is kind. It is not jealous, love is not pompous, it is not inflated, it is not rude, it is not quick-tempered, it does not brood over injury, it does not rejoice over wrongdoing but rejoices with the truth. It bears all things, believes all things, hopes all things, endures all things. Love never fails."

1 Corinthians 13:4-8a

Themes: Love, God, Adam, Eve, Beauty, Patience, Affection, Romance, Sex, Lust

144. REMOTE CONTROL IN THE PURSE

"Cash, check or charge?" I asked, after folding items the woman wished to purchase. As she fumbled for her wallet, I noticed a remote control for a television set in her purse.

"So, do you always carry your TV remote?" I asked.

"No," she replied, "but my husband refused to come shopping with me, so I figured this was the most legal evil thing I could do to him."

* * *

Sometime people punish the very same people they love. They take revenge on their spouses for silly reasons. It is human nature to take revenge when one is hurt. But remember it is the strong person who forgives. When you forgive, you are set free. You are released from bitterness and anger. Then the healing process begins.

The Bible says: "When you stand to pray, forgive anyone against whom you have a grievance, so that your heavenly Father may in turn forgive you your transgressions" (Mark 11:25). If you expect God to forgive, you have to be also forgiving. Jesus was able to forgive his executioners.

"Revenge is not always sweet, once it is consummated we feel inferior to our victim." – Emile M. Cioran

"There is no revenge so complete as forgiveness." – Josh Billings

Themes: Forgiveness, Pardon, Sympathy, Compassion, Revenge, Hatred, Retaliation, Anger, Bitterness.

145. UNDERSTANDING TRINITY

A Bishop was visiting a parish for Confirmation and asked the young people: Who can explain the meaning of Trinity?"

A girl from the back said: "It is one God in three persons."

The bishop could not hear the answer well and so he said: "I don't understand, please repeat."

The girl replied: "You are not expected to understand because it is a mystery."

* * *

The famous prayer of St. Francis of Assisi says: "Grant that I may not so much seek to be consoled, as to console; to be understood, as to understand; to be loved, as to love." Seek first to understand, than to be understood. You can fall into the trap of so seriously wanting to get your point across, you forget to listen to the person you are speaking to. Try your best to understand the other. Good relationships are built on understanding. When you have issues in understanding others, ask yourself: "Why are they doing what they are doing?"

People don't always want advice. What they need is a hand to hold, an ear to listen, and a heart to understand them. Where there is love there is understanding.

"Knowing your own darkness is the best method for dealing with the darknesses of other people." – Carl Jung

"You never understand a person until you consider things from his point of view." – Harper Lee

Themes: God, Trinity, Confirmation, Bishop, Youth, Young People, Relationship, Understanding, Listening, Mystery, Relationship.

146. THE SECRET OF THE RITUAL

Every time a new Pope is elected, there's a whole lot of rituals and ceremonies that have to be gone through, in accordance with tradition. Well there's one tradition that very few people know about.

Shortly after the new Pope is enthroned, the Chief Rabbi seeks an audience. He is shown into the Pope's presence, whereupon he presents him with a silver tray bearing a velvet cushion. On top of the cushion is an ancient, shriveled parchment envelope.

The Pope symbolically stretches out his arm in a gesture of rejection.

The Chief Rabbi then retires, taking the envelope with him and does not return until the next Pope is elected. Pope Francis was intrigued by this ritual, whose origins were unknown to him. He instructed the best scholars of the Vatican to research it, but they came up with nothing. When the time came and the Chief Rabbi was shown into his presence, he faithfully enacted the ritual of rejection but, as the Chief Rabbi turned to leave, he called him back.

"My brother," the Holy Father whispered, "I must confess that we Catholics are ignorant of the meaning of this ritual enacted for centuries between us and you, the representative of the Jewish people. I have to ask you, what is it all about?"

The Chief Rabbi shrugs and replies: "But we have no more idea than you do. The origin of the ceremony is lost in the traditions of ancient history."

The Pope said: "Let us retire to my private chambers and enjoy a glass of wine together, then, with your agreement, we shall open the envelope and discover at last the secret."

The Chief Rabbi agreed.

Fortified in their resolve by the wine, they gingerly pried open the curling parchment envelope and with trembling fingers, the Chief Rabbi reached inside and extracted a folded sheet of similarly ancient paper. As the Pope peered over his shoulder, he slowly opened it.

They both gasped with shock.

It was the check for the Last Supper.

* * *

It was at the Last Supper that Jesus instituted the Holy Eucharist and the ministerial priesthood. He told the apostles at the table: "Do this in memory of me."

Each time a Holy Mass is celebrated, the priests recall the words of Jesus Christ at the Last Supper. The bread and wine offered truly become the body and blood of Christ. That is called transubstantiation and is a doctrine of the Roman Catholic Church.

The "Real Presence" is the term referring to Christ's actual presence in the elements of the bread and wine that have been transubstantiated.

"This is the wonderful truth my dear friends: the Word which became flesh two thousand years ago, is present today in the Eucharist." – St. John Paul II

"Whoever eats my flesh and drinks my blood has eternal life and I will raise him on the last day." – John 6:54

Themes: Eucharist, Mass, Last Supper, Jesus Christ, Transubstantiation, Holy Communion, Rabbi, Pope, Priesthood, Church.

147. Fish and Chips

Lost on a rainy night, a nun stumbled across a monastery and requests shelter there.

Fortunately, she's just in time for dinner and was treated to the best fish and chips she had ever tasted.

After dinner, she went into the kitchen to thank the chefs. She was met by two of the Brothers.

The first one says, "Hello, I am brother Michael, and this is Brother Charles."

"I'm very pleased to meet you," replies the nun. "I just wanted to thank you for the wonderful dinner.

The fish and chips were the best I've ever had. Out of curiosity, who cooked what?"

Brother Charles replied, "Well, I'm the fish friar."

She turned to the other Brother and says "then you must be..."

"Yes, I'm afraid I'm the chip monk."

* * *

Hospitality is love in action. It is showing the guest that you do care for them and make them feel that they are at home. In some cultures, they consider guests as gods visiting them and they go out of their way to honor them.

When you show hospitality to anyone, you are saying that person matters and is important to you. The kindness you render will come back to you in one way or another eventually.

"Do not neglect hospitality, for through it some have unknowingly entertained angels." – Hebrews 13:2

"Hospitality means making a space for others, not so that we can exploit them or get something from them or even so that we can make them become like us. It is showing them the same kind of grace and mercy, the same presence, that God has given us." – Elaine Heath

Themes: Hospitality, Warmth, Friendliness, Love, Guests, Monks, Monastery, Care, Kindness, Angels, God.

148. GIFTS FOR THE MOTHER

Four brothers left home for college, and they became successful doctors and lawyers and prospered.

Some years later, they chatted after having dinner together. They discussed the gifts they were able to give their elderly mother who lived far away in another city.

The first said, "I had a big house built for Mama."

The second said, "I had a hundred thousand dollar theater built in the house."

The third said, "I had my Mercedes dealer deliver an SL600 to her."

The fourth said, "You know how Mamma loved reading the Bible and you know she can't read anymore because she can't see very well. I met this preacher who told me about a parrot that can recite the entire bible. It took twenty preachers 12 years to teach him. I had to pledge to contribute $100,000 a year for twenty years to the church, but it was worth it. Mamma just has to name the chapter and verse and the parrot will recite it."

The other brothers were impressed.

After the holidays Mom sent out her Thank You notes. She wrote:

"Milton, the house you built is so huge. I live in only one room, but I have to clean the whole house. Thanks anyway."

"Marvin, I am too old to travel. I stay home; I have my groceries delivered, so I never use the Mercedes. The thought was good. Thanks."

"Michael, you gave me and expensive theater with Dolby sound, it could hold 50 people, but all of my friends are dead, I've lost my hearing and I'm nearly blind. I'll never use it. Thank you for the gesture just the same."

"Dearest Melvin, you were the only son to have the good sense to give a little thought to your gift. The chicken was delicious. Thank you."

* * *

When you get a gift, don't just focus on the wrapping or on the bag. That is not the gift. The true gift is the person of the giver. He or she is a blessing in your life.

Be a gift or a blessing for others. Many people prefer or are comfortable giving gifts than receiving them. Giving may be more rewarding than receiving on many ways. It is the thought that counts. Charitable giving will make you feel good. Give practical gifts.

"A gift consists not in what is done or given, but in the intention of the giver or doer." – Seneca

"A wise lover values not so much the gift of the lover as the love of the giver." – Thomas a Kempis

Themes: Gifts, Presents, Offerings, Aids, Mother, Generosity, Stewardship, Brothers, House, Vehicle, Travel, Bible.

149. MEDICINE AND MECHANICS

A mechanic was removing a cylinder head from the motor of a Harley motorcycle when he spotted a well-known heart surgeon in his shop. The surgeon was there waiting for the service manager to come take a look at his bike. The mechanic shouted across the garage, "Hey, Doc, can I ask you a question?"

The surgeon, a bit surprised, walked over to the mechanic working on the motorcycle. The mechanic straightened up, wiped his hands on a rag and asked, "So Doc, look at this engine. I open its heart, take valves out, fix them, put them back in, and when I finish, it works just like new. So how come I get such a small salary and you get the really big bucks, when you and I are doing basically the same work?"

The surgeon paused, smiled and leaned over, and whispered to the mechanic, "Try doing it with the engine running."

* * *

When you are fully alive, you are honoring your creator. Live your ordinary life in an extraordinary way. Do not just exist; be open to some adventure in life.

Do what you are created to do. You are unique and you have a mission on earth to fulfill. Every new day is a gift from God; live as if it is your last day alive. Make the best of it by giving and receiving.

Prepare for eternity by living every moment of your life joyously. Spend time in nature, feel the wind on your face and smell the fresh air. Connect with another human being and make that person smile.

"Glory of God is man fully alive." – Saint Irenaeus

"Do not take life too seriously. You will never get out of it alive." – Elbert Hubbard

Themes: Life, Doctor, Medicine, Health, Healing, Surgery, Surgeon, Mechanic, God, Creator, Eternity, Nature.

150. THE MIRROR ISSUE

After living in the remote wilderness of Kentucky all his life, an old hillbilly decided it was time to visit the big city.

In one of the stores, he picked up a mirror and looked in it. Not knowing what it was, he remarked, "How about that! Here's a picture of my daddy."

He bought the "picture," but on the way home he remembered his wife, Lizy, didn't like his father. So he hung it in the barn, and every morning before leaving for the fields, he would go there and look at it.

Lizy began to get suspicious of these many trips to the barn.

One day after her husband left, she searched the barn and found the mirror.

As she looked into the glass, she fumed, "So that's the ugly witch he's running around with!"

* * *

You have an image of yourself, which is called self-image. It is the idea you have about your abilities, appearances, and personality. It is important to have a good self-image of yourself. Many people have a poor or bad self-image. Self-image has a very strong bearing on your happiness, and your attitude on life can affect those around you. If you display a positive self-image, people will be more likely to see you as an optimistic and capable person.

Positive and realistic self-image is vital. Ask yourself: What's your internal voice saying? You can change the distortions in the mirror and have a healthier view of yourself. A healthy self-image begins with learning to accept and love yourself. It also means being accepted and loved by others.

"Our self-image, strongly held, essentially determines what we become."

– Maxwell Maltz

"To be beautiful means to be yourself. You don't need to be

accepted by others. You need to accept yourself." – Thich Nhat Hanh

Themes: Self-image, Self Esteem, Happiness, Attitude, Husband, Wife, Witch.

151. NUNS AT THE BASEBALL GAME

Sitting behind a couple of nuns at a baseball game (whose habits partially blocked the view), three men decided to badger the nuns in effort to get them to move.

In a very loud voice, the first guy said, "I think I'm going to move to Utah, there are only 100 nuns living there."

The second guy spoke up and said, "I want to go to Montana, there are only 50 nuns living there".

The third guy said, "I want to go to Idaho, there are only 25 nuns living there."

One of the nuns turned around, looked at the men, and in a very sweet, calm voice said, "Why don't you go to hell? There aren't any nuns there."

* * *

There are people who live consecrated lives for the sake of the Gospel. Religious orders have flourished in the Catholic Church. Consecrated persons are to leave some aspect of the world such as marriage and following secular goals to put themselves at the service of brothers and sisters.

Religious men and women take the vows of poverty, chastity

and obedience. Usually they live in communities. That entails discipline and sacrifice.

Nearly all religious orders and communities offer ways for you to share in their life and ministry. Communities welcome your support.

"Today's religious men and women need to be prophetic, 'capable of waking up the world,' of showing they are a special breed who 'have something to say' to the world today." – Pope Francis

"Religious live more purely, they fall more rarely, they rise more speedily, they are aided more powerfully, they live more peacefully, they die more securely, and they are rewarded more abundantly." – St. Bernard of Clairvaux

Themes: Religious, Orders, Vows, Chastity, Poverty, Obedience, Nuns, Consecrated Life, Baseball, Habits, Gospel.

152. DAD'S WARNING

An older Jewish gentleman was on the operating table awaiting surgery and he insisted that his son, a renowned surgeon, perform the operation. As he was about to get the anesthesia he asked to speak to his son.

"Yes, Dad, what is it?"

"Don't be nervous, son; do your best and just remember, if it doesn't go well, if something happens to me, your mother is going to come and live with you and your wife ... "

* * *

"Honor thy father and thy mother" is one of the Ten Commandments in the Bible. You have to have respect and esteem for their position of being parents. Honoring means to revere and value them.

Here are some ways that you can show honor to your parents. You have to obey your parents when you are under their care. You can pray for your parents. You can help them in whatever way you can. Show appreciation for what they have done for you. Forgive your parents for their wrongdoing.

"A child who is allowed to be disrespectful to his parents will not have true respect for anyone." – Billy Graham

"Let parents bequeath to their children not riches, but the spirit of reverence."

Themes: Commandments, Parents, Children, Father, Mother, Dad, Son, Honor, Respect, Doctor, Forgiveness, Obedience, Appreciation, Reverence.

153. Name the Restaurant

An elderly couple had dinner at another couple's house, and after eating, the wives left the table and went into the kitchen.

The two gentlemen were talking, and one said, "Last night we went out to a new restaurant and it was really great. I would recommend it very highly". The other man said, "What is the name of the restaurant?"

The first man thought and thought and finally said, "What is the name of that flower you give to someone you love? You know... the one that's red and has thorns."

"Do you mean a rose?"

"Yes, that's the one," replied the man. He then turned towards the kitchen and yelled, "Rose, what's the name of that restaurant we went to last night?"

* * *

If you have a healthy brain, you will have a strong memory. Regular exercise and adequate sleep are vital to harness the power of your brain. Studies have shown that having meaningful relationship and robust support system are important not only for emotional health, but also for brain health. Laughter is the best medicine not only for the body but also for the brain and memory.

Memories don't change and that is the reason why people hold onto them. They are the timeless treasures of the heart. Some memories can never be replaced.

"Memory is a way of holding onto the things you love, the things you are, the things you never want to lose." – Kevin Arnold

"Yesterday is but today's memory, and tomorrow is today's dream."

– Khalil Gibran

Themes: Memory, Gentlemen, Restaurant, Rose, Relationship, Exercise, Sleep, Laughter.

154. CAR BREAK-IN

An elderly Floridian called 911 on her cell phone to report that her car has been broken into. She is hysterical as she explains her situation to the dispatcher: "They've stolen the stereo, the steering wheel, the brake pedal and even the accelerator!" she cried. The dispatcher said, "Stay calm. An officer is on the way."

A few minutes later, the officer radios in his report. He says: "She got in the back-seat by mistake."

* * *

People tend to blame others without knowing all the facts. Rash judgment, running down friends and jumping to conclusions are signs of immaturity. Ask before you draw conclusions. Rash judgment is when you rush to decide without enough evidence. Typically because you are led by emotions and make snap decisions when you don't like what is before you. The problem with assumptions is that you believe they are the truth.

Cultivate the skills of correct understanding of context, keen observation, and careful actions to find the facts.

It is said that people will question all the good things they hear about you but believe all the bad things without a second thought.

"Real magic in relationships means an absence of judgment of others." – Wayne Dyer

"It often happens that things are other than what they seem, and you can get yourself into trouble by jumping to conclusions." – Paul Auster

Themes: Knowledge, Facts, Rash Judgment, Jumping to conclusions, Context, Observation, Relationship.

155. CONFUSION OF THE RETIREES

Three retirees, each with a hearing loss, were playing golf one fine March day. One remarked to the other, "Windy, isn't it?"

"No," the second man replied, "it's Thursday."

And the third man chimed in, "So am I. Let's have a beer."

* * *

You hear what you want to hear. You get what you want to get. Your thoughts become things. You can change your future by changing your thoughts.

In a day you have about 50,000 to 70,000 thoughts. Your predominant thoughts will become reality for you. So be very careful about what you think. Think about what you want to have manifested. If you are happy and grateful you can attract whatever you want, be it prosperity, wellness, relationship, success or happiness in life. The *law of attraction* says that you can attract positive or negative things by focusing on positive or negative thoughts.

"What we think, we become." – Buddha

"Your thoughts are the architects of your destiny." – David O. McKay

Themes: Thoughts, Hearing, Manifestation, Law of Attraction, Positive, Negative, Destiny, Retirees.

156. Miracle of Turning Water into Wine

Jesus, his mother Mary, his foster father Joseph and the disciples were invited to a wedding feast in Cana. Jesus worked his first miracle there by turning water into wine. An abundance of wine flowed at the party. According to a story, Joseph had a bit too much of that.

The next day, Joseph woke up with a bad headache resulting from his over indulgence of the wine the previous night. So he called out to Mary his wife and said: "Please bring me a glass of water for me to drink." Then he added: "Don't allow that son of ours to touch it!"

* * *

Jesus worked many miracles while he was on earth such as healing people, raising the dead to life, multiplying bread and fish, nature miracles, etc. Some of the miracles were performed by touch while others were done from a distance.

Jesus is a living God who is very much alive and is present in you. He can perform miracles in your life today.

Jesus often demanded faith from the people before he worked the miracles. If you have profound faith in Him, He will do the same miracles for you today.

"Miracles are a retelling in small letters of the very same story which is written across the world in letters too large for some of us to see." – C.S. Lewis

"Miracles are not contrary to nature, but only contrary to what we know about nature." – St. Augustine

Themes: Jesus, Mary, Joseph, Miracles, Wine, Wedding, Party, Husband, Wife, Faith.

157. LIKE A NEWBORN BABY

Two elderly gentlemen from a retirement center were sitting on a bench under a tree when one turns to the other and says: "Slim, I'm 83 years old now and I'm just full of aches and pains. I know you're about my age. How do you feel?"

Slim says, "I feel just like a new-born baby."

"Really ? Like a newborn baby?"

"Yep. No hair, no teeth, and I think I just wet my pants."

* * *

There is some similarity between childhood and old age; in both those stages of life you become helpless and are dependent on others.

Good wine gets better and better as it ages. So also we get better and better as wrinkles start forming and we can get senior discounts. With age comes wisdom, but sometimes age comes alone. Have lots of good memories to savor.

"Some are born great, some achieve greatness, and some have greatness thrust upon them." – William Shakespeare

"The secret of genius is to carry the spirit of the child into old age, which means never lose your enthusiasm." – Aldous Huxley

Themes: Childhood, Old age, Newborn, Baby, Children, Birth, Death, Aging, Genius.

158. JUMPING RED LIGHT

Two elderly women were out driving in a large car, both could barely see over the dashboard. As they were cruising along, they came to an intersection. The stoplight was red, but they just went on through. The woman in the passenger seat thought to herself "I must be losing it. I could have sworn we just went through a red light."

After a few more minutes, they came to another intersection and the light was red. Again, they went right through. The woman in the passenger seat was almost sure that the light had been red but was really concerned that she was losing it. She was getting nervous.

At the next intersection, sure enough, the light was red and they went on through. So, she turned to the other woman and said, "Mildred, did you know that we just ran through three red lights in a row? You could have killed us both!"

Mildred turned to her and said, "Oh my! Am I driving?"

* * *

Self-awareness is knowing your mind, body and soul. It is the key to your success. Knowing yourself is a lifelong quest. Self-awareness can lead you to self-acceptance and self-love.

Self-awareness is important because when you have the better knowledge of yourself, you are able to enjoy your uniqueness. That will help your self-improvement too.

Awareness of what you are doing is vital. People do certain things, without even knowing that they are doing them and why they are doing them. Do what you love most.

"He who knows others is wise. He who knows himself is enlightened." – Lao Tzu

"Your vision will only become clear when you can look into your own heart. Who looks outside, dreams; who looks inside awakens." – Carl Jung

Themes: Awareness, Self-awareness, Self-acceptance, Self-love, Uniqueness, Knowledge, Vision, Elderly, Red Light, Stoplight, Driver.

159. MONEY FOR AFTERLIFE

There was a man who had worked all of his life, had saved all of his money, and was a real miser when it came to his money. Just before he died, he said to his wife, "When I die, I want you to take all my money and put it in the casket with me. I want to take my money to the afterlife with me."

And so he got his wife to promise him with all of her heart that when he died, she would put all of the money in the casket with him.

Well, he died. He was stretched out in the casket, his wife was sitting there in black, and her friend was sitting next to her. When they finished the ceremony, just before the undertakers got ready to close the casket, the wife said, "Wait just a minute!" She had a box with her; she came over with the box and put it in the casket. Then the undertakers locked the casket down, and they rolled it away.

So her friend said, "Girl, I know you weren't fool enough to put all that money in there with your husband." The loyal wife replied, "Listen,

I'm a Christian, I can't go back on my word. I promised him that I was going to put that money in that casket with him."

"You mean to tell me you put all that money in the casket with him?"

"I sure did," said the wife. "I got it all together, put it into my account and wrote him a check. If he can cash it, he can spend it."

* * *

Be generous with your time, talent and treasure. When you give freely do not expect anything in return. But that will give greater happiness, health and satisfaction. You can't take your wealth to the grave. You don't see U-hauls after the hearse.

The Dead Sea is dead because it only receives water and nothing flows out of it. You too are dead if you do not give anything.

Do not ask yourself: "What is in it for me?" but ask yourself:

"How may I serve." There is more joy in giving than receiving.

"If you can't feed a hundred people, then just feed one."
– Blessed Mother Teresa

"We make a living by what we get, but we make a life by what we give." – Winston Churchill

Themes: Generosity, Giving, Loving, Charity, Selfishness, Money, Afterlife, Miser, Husband, Wife, Christian.

160. LEMON REMEDY

An old gent moved into a retirement community where good-looking, eligible men are at a premium. After he had been there for a week he went to confession and said, "Bless me, Father, for I have sinned. Last week I had my way with seven different women."

The priest said, "Take seven lemons, squeeze them into a glass and drink the juice without pausing."

"Will that cleanse me of my sins, Father?"

"No," replied the priest, "but it'll wipe that grin off your face."

* * *

Confession of sins to a priest is a Catholic practice. You need a lot of courage and humility to go to the confessional and admit your wrongdoings and beg for God's mercy. When you confess sincerely your failures and you are repentant, not only does God forgive but also you feel liberated. Psychologically you are set free.

Once you experience God's forgiveness, you have to forgive yourself. Many people know that God forgives them but they have a hard time forgiving themselves. Be gracious to yourself and pardon yourself.

Just as you are forgiven by God, remember to forgive others. Let go of anger, grudges, resentment and bitterness. Forgiveness of others will bring about happiness, health and peace.

"Confession of errors is like a broom which sweeps away dirt and leaves the surface brighter and clearer. I feel stronger for confession." – Mahatma Gandhi

"Three conditions are necessary for Penance: contrition, which is sorrow for sin, together with a purpose of amendment; confession of sins without any omission; and satisfaction by means of good works." – Thomas Aquinas

Themes: Confession, Priest, Forgiveness, Courage, humility, Sins, Mercy, God, Freedom, Anger, Bitterness, Women.

161. DEATH IN HOLY LAND

A man, his wife, and mother-in-law went on vacation to the Holy Land.

While they were there the mother-in-law passed away. The undertaker told them, "You can have her shipped home for $5,000, or you can bury her here in the Holy Land for $150.00."

The man thought about it and told him he would just have her shipped home.

The undertaker asked, "Why?" Why would you spend $5,000 to ship your mother-in-law home, when it would be wonderful to be buried here and spend only $150.00?"

The man said, "A man died here 2000 years ago, he was buried here and three days later he rose from the dead. I just can't take that chance."

* * *

Most people believe in afterlife. With death, life does not come to an end. Death is only a passage from this life to the next life. Souls live on in eternity forever. Live in the hope of resurrection.

It is in the resurrection of Christ and his promise of resurrection that you have the guarantee of your resurrection. For Christ has said: "I am the resurrection and the life; whoever believes in me, even if he dies, will live, and everyone who lives and believes in me will never die." (John 11:25-26)

The degree to which you believe in the resurrection of the dead will determine the way that you presently live. If you believe that this world is not the end, you will look at this life very differently.

"Death is the golden key that opens the palace of eternity." – John Milton

"We are an Easter people and Alleluia is our song." – St. Augustine of Hippo

Themes: Resurrection, Death, Afterlife, Eternity, Souls, Christ, Belief, Undertaker, Funeral Director, Mortuary, Holy Land, Mother-in-law.

162. The Branch Manager

A blonde gets ready, wears a formal dress, goes out, climbs a tree and sits on the branch regularly. A friend asked why she did that.

Blonde: "I have been promoted to branch manager."

* * *

Jesus says: "I am the vine, you are the branches. Whoever remains in me and I in him will bear much fruit, because without me you can do nothing." (John 15:5) The vine and the branches is a metaphor to show how one should "remain" in Christ. It is not enough to remain with him, but you must bear fruit.

When you draw closer to God, He will come closer to you. Attachment to Christ will demand certain detachment from the world. Let go and let God. Pruning is an essential part of growing fruit-bearing branches. Remove everything that is contrary to the Gospel.

A relationship with God is the most significant relationship you can have. Have faith in Him and everything will turn out fine. Your active participation in the liturgy will help you in your relationship with Him. He relates to you in a most loving way. Just the same way, relate well with your brothers and sisters.

"When we enter into a personal relationship with Jesus Christ, something wonderful happens: God begins to change our desires and we want to be more like Him." – Joyce Meyer

"Every relationship for a Christian is an opportunity to love another person like God has loved us." – Joshua Harris

*Themes: Blonde, Branch Manager, Vine, Attachment, De-
tachment, Intimacy, Relationship, Gospel, God, Jesus Christ,
Christian, Love.*

163. PARTYING ALONE

Patrick was spotted driving along the highway at a steady
speed, when he suddenly signaled a right turn and pulled off
onto the shoulder. He quickly jumped out of the car and opened
the trunk. From a large bag, he produced a party hat, streamers,
a bottle of lemonade, sandwiches and a cake.

After eating the food and drinking the lemonade, he launched
into a little Irish jig. The whole proceedings lasted about fifteen
minutes, after which he got back in his car and drove off.

Curious, the police followed him at a distance and half an
hour later, they saw him stop and repeat the whole procedure.
This was too much for the officers, so they decided to check
him out.

"Can we ask you the reason for all the stops and the food,
drink and Irish jigs?" one of the officers asked.

"Well, sir," explained Patrick, "I'm on the company's
outing."

"But you're the only one here," argued the officer.

"Yes, I know," replied Patrick. "I'm self-employed!"

* * *

When you are self-employed, you are your own boss. That

demands great discipline and responsibility. But then you can do your dream job and can be passionate about it.

Self-reliance helps you to assume responsibility and make your own decisions. You will be able to trust your instincts and form your own opinions. Since people are not always going to be there for you, you have to learn to handle things on your own.

"Do not go where the path may lead, go instead where there is no path and leave a trail." – Ralph Waldo Emerson

"The three great essentials to achieve anything worthwhile are: Hard work, Stick-to-itiveness, and Common sense." – Thomas A. Edison

Themes: Self-employment, Self-reliance, Company outing, Party, Police, Boss, Responsibility, Decision making, Work, Labor.

164. SEIZE THE OPPORTUNITY

An elderly couple was on a cruise and it was really stormy. They were standing on the back of the boat watching the moon, when a wave came up and washed the old woman overboard.

They searched for days and couldn't find her, so the captain sent the old man back to shore with the promise that he would notify him as soon as they found something.

Three weeks went by and finally the old man got a fax from the boat. It read: "Sir, sorry to inform you, we found your wife dead at the bottom of the ocean. We hauled her up to the deck and attached to her butt was an oyster and in it was a pearl worth $50,000! Please advice."

The old man faxed back: "Send me the pearl and re-bait the trap."

* * *

Seize the opportunities because they may not be there again. Take advantage of the situation when offered. If you wait too long for the perfect moment, the perfect may not come.

Be prepared for all kinds of opportunities however, you may never be totally ready. Successful people have all seen and grabbed opportunities that came to them. Every moment is an opportunity to improve, don't waste it.

"If someone offers you an amazing opportunity and you're not sure you can do it, say yes – then learn how to do it later." – Richard Branson

"Your purpose on earth is to participate in this human experience and to seize the opportunity within each day to reveal the greatest version of yourself." – Steve Maraboli

Themes: Seize the Opportunity, Cruise, Elderly, Pearl, Wealth, Success, Purpose, Human Experience.

165. SECOND CHANCE

A funeral service is being held for a woman who has just passed away. At the end of the service, the pallbearers were carrying the casket out when they accidentally bumped into a wall, jarring the casket.

They heard a faint moan. They opened the casket and found that the woman is actually alive!

She lived for ten more years, and then died.

Once again, a ceremony is held, and at the end of it, the pallbearers were again carrying out the casket. As they carried the casket towards the door, the husband cries out, "Watch that wall!"

* * *

Everyone makes mistakes. Children fall many times before they learn to walk. If you are not allowed to make mistakes, why are there erasers on the pencil?

Sometimes people are not ready for the first chance. God gives second chances and everyone deserves them. Sometimes people bounce back. If you learn from the mistakes, second chances can work out better. A second chance does not guarantee success.

Sometimes good people make bad choices; it doesn't mean they are bad. It means they are human.

"Until we have seen someone's darkness we don't really know who they are. Until we have forgiven someone's darkness, we don't really know what love is." – Marianne Williamson

"The good thing about failing is that you get a second chance to do better." – Omelia Lalman

Themes: Second Chance, Opportunities, Choices, Darkness, Failures, Mistakes, God, People, Human, Funeral, Life, Death, Life, Watch.

166. ROAD PARKING

One winter morning a couple was listening to the radio while eating breakfast. They hear the announcer say, "We are going to have 8 to 10 inches of snow today. You must park your car on the even - numbered side of the street, so the snowplows can get through." Norman's wife goes out and moves her car.

A week later while they are eating breakfast again, the radio announcer says, "We are expecting 10 to 12 inches of snow today. You must park your car on the odd-numbered side of the street, so the snowplows can get through." Norman's wife goes out and moves her car again.

The next week they are again having breakfast, when the radio announcer says "We are expecting 12 to 14 inches of snow today. You must park ..." Then the electric power goes out. Norman's wife is very upset, and with a worried look on her face she says, "Honey, I don't know what to do. Which side of the street do I need to park on so the snowplows can get through?"

With the love and understanding in his voice that all men who are married to Blondes exhibit, Norman says ... "Why don't you just leave it in the garage this time?"

* * *

"Can't see the forest for the trees" is an expression used for a person who is so involved in the details of a situation who fails to see the situation as a whole. See the big picture. It is not enough to know how and what to do, but know why you do what you do.

Enlarge your vision. If you have a vision, you will see the big picture. It is what you see, what you will get. Then you will seize every opportunity and expand the possibilities. Have the aptitude to see the impact of your work.

"The smallest change in perspective can transform a life. What tiny attitude adjustment might turn your world around?" – Oprah Winfrey

"We don't see things as they are. We see things as we are." – Anais Nin

Themes: Vision, Mission, Big Picture, Forest, Trees, Work, Labor, Blonde.

167. DEMONSTRATION OF THE DIFFERENCE

A Lawyer runs a stop sign and gets pulled over by a Sheriff's Deputy. He thinks that he is smarter than the Deputy because he is sure that he has a better education. He decides to prove this to himself and have some fun at the deputy's expense.

Deputy says, "License and registration, please."

Lawyer says, "What for?"

Deputy says, "You didn't come to a complete stop at the stop sign."

Lawyer says, "I slowed down, and no one was coming."

Deputy says, "You still didn't come to a complete stop. License and registration, please."

Lawyer says, "What's the difference?"

Deputy says, "The difference is, you have to come to a complete stop, that's the law. License and registration, please!"

Lawyer says, "If you can show me the legal difference between slow down and stop, I'll give you my license and registration and you give me the ticket. If not, you let me go and no ticket."

Deputy says, "Exit your vehicle, sir."

At this point, the Deputy takes out his nightstick and starts beating the ever-loving crap out of the Lawyer and says:

"Do you want me to stop or just slow down?"

* * *

"Action speaks louder than words." What one does is more important than what one says. Mere words are meaningless unless translated into actions. So don't just tell, but show.

Faith is not taught but caught. Children will usually imitate their parents. It is more important how you live your life and rather than what you tell your children to do.

People will judge you by your actions, not your intentions. Mahatma Gandhi used to say: "My life is my message." What message do you give out through your life?

"Well done is better than well said." – Benjamin Franklin

"Preach at all times, use words if necessary." – St. Francis of Assisi

Themes: Actions, Words, Faith, Lawyer, Sheriff, Police, Officer, Deputy, Driver, Message, Preacher, Life.

168. SHAKEN UP

A passenger in a taxi leaned over to ask the driver a question and tapped him on the shoulder. The driver screamed, lost control of the cab, nearly hit a bus, drove up over the curb, and stopped just inches from a large plate glass window.

For a few moments everything was silent in the cab, and then the still shaking driver said, "I'm sorry but you scared the daylights out of me." The frightened passenger, apologized to the driver, and said he didn't realize a mere tap on the shoulder could frighten him so much.

The driver replied, "No, no, I'm sorry, it's entirely my fault. Today is my first day driving a cab ... I've been driving a hearse for the last 23 years."

* * *

Fear can paralyze one. People suffer from all types of fears. There is the fear of the future, fear of death, fear of rejection, fear of failure, fear of losing health, fearing of losing loved ones, fear of losing jobs etc.

You cannot control external events but you can control your mind. If you live in fear you will lose what you have in the present. Fear is the main enemy of accomplishment because it makes you inactive. Imagine positive futures and prepare for peaceful implementation.

Remember that you are never alone. The God who created you and loves you very dearly is always with you. Have unlimited trust and confidence that He will take care of you.

"Fear is an idea-crippling, experience-crushing, success-stalling inhibitor inflicted only by yourself." – Stephanie Melish

"Do the things you fear most and the death of fear is certain." – Mark Twain

Themes: Fear, Anxiety, Courage, Future, People, Mind, Thoughts, God, Death, Rejection, Taxi, Cab, Driver, Hearse, Passenger.

169. THANK GOD

There's this guy who had been lost and walking in the desert for about two weeks. One hot day, he sees the home of a missionary. Tired and weak, he crawls up to the house and collapses on the doorstep. The missionary finds him and nurses him back to health. Feeling better, the man asks the missionary for directions to the nearest town. On his way out of the backdoor, he sees his horse. He goes back into the house and asks the missionary, "Could I borrow your horse and give it back when I reach the town?"

The missionary says, "Sure but there is a special thing about this horse. You have to say 'Thank God' to make it go and 'Amen' to make it stop." Not paying much attention, the man says, "Sure, ok."

So he gets on the horse and says, "Thank God" and the horse starts walking. Then he says, "Thank God, thank God," and the horse starts trotting. Feeling really brave, the man says, "Thank God, thank God, thank God, thank God, thank God" and the horse just takes off. Pretty soon he sees this cliff coming up and he's doing everything he can to make the horse stop.

"Whoa, stop, hold on!" Finally he remembers, "Amen!"

The horse stops 4 inches from the cliff. Then the man leans back in the saddle and says, "Thank God."

* * *

We are all creatures of habit. There are good habits and bad habits. It is difficult to break habits. If you remove the first letter from "Habit", "abit" remains. If you remove "a" from that, "bit" remains. If you remove "b" from that, "it" still remains.

It is said that bad habits are like a comfortable bed, easy to get into, but hard to get out of. It is the bad habits that will destroy you; your good habits will save you.

If you want to take control of your life, take control of your habits. The secret of success is having a good routine of doing certain things to achieve your goal.

"We are what we repeatedly do. Excellence, then, is not an act, but a habit." – Aristotle

"First we form habits, then they form us. Conquer your bad habits, or they'll eventually conquer you." – Rob Gilbert

Themes: Habits, Routine, Excellence, Customs, Behaviors, Missionary, Horse, Gratitude, Thanks, Desert, Amen.

170. LET GO OF THE ROPE

There was a flood and people were stranded on a tiny island. A helicopter came to rescue them. Eleven people scrambled onto the rope and were hanging under the helicopter. It happened that 10 were men and one was a woman. 11 were too many for the helicopter to carry and so the captain announced: "One of you have to let go or else all will perish." There was a dead silence.

They were not able to choose that person, but then the only woman made a very touching speech. She said: "I am a mother, I am used to making a lot of sacrifices for the family. I am used to giving up everything for my husband and kids and for men in general without ever getting anything in return. So I am ready to let go off the rope." As soon as she finished her speech, all the men applauded.

* * *

"Mother" is the sweetest word in any language. Most people think that their mother is the best. Mothers are very important in the life and growth of a child. A mother understands what a child does not say. Children learn a lot of things from her.

Mothers make a lot of sacrifices for their children. Often mothers eat only once the children have eaten. Mothers are the emotional strength of the family.

Motherhood has the greatest possible influence in human life. Being a mother is tougher than anyone can tell you; but also more gratifying than anyone will ever tell you. ·

"The natural state of motherhood is unselfishness. When you become a mother you are no longer the center of your own universe. You relinquish that position to your children." – Jessica Lange

"Motherhood is near to divinity. It is the highest, holiest service to be assumed by mankind." – Howard W. Hunter

Themes: Mother, Motherhood, Sacrifices, Influence, Center, Child, Children, Babies, Divinity, Mankind, Helicopter, Man, Woman.

171. THE SILENT TREATMENT

A man and his wife were having some problems at home and were giving each other the silent treatment. Suddenly, the man realized that the next day, he would need his wife to wake him at 5:00 a.m. for an early morning business flight. Not wanting to be the first to break the silence and lose, he wrote on a piece of paper, "Please wake me up at 5:00 a.m." He left it where he knew she would find it.

The next morning, the man woke up, only to discover it was 9:00 a.m.

He had missed his flight. Furious, he was about to go and see why his wife hadn't wakened him, when he noticed a piece of paper by the bed.

The paper said, "It is 5:00 a.m. Wake up."

* * *

People sometimes try to punish the very same people whom they love. When they are upset, it is often the silent treatment. Tit for tat is not healthy in marriage.

Jesus Christ taught the importance of forgiveness saying: "You have heard that it was said, "An eye for an eye and a tooth for a tooth.' But I say to you, offer no resistance to one who is evil. When someone strikes you on your right cheek, turn the other one to him as well." (Matthew 5: 38-39)

It takes a tough person to say sorry, and an even tougher person to forgive. Forgiveness is not only good spiritually but also good for your physical wellbeing. You will have less anxiety and stress and lower your blood pressure. Let go off the grudges.

"An eye for an eye will leave the whole world blind." – Mahatma Gandhi

"You have the power to take away someone's happiness by refusing to forgive. That someone is you." – Alan Cohen

Themes: Forgiveness, Pardon, Healing, Mercy, Love, Punishment, Spirituality, Anger, Hatred, Grudges, Anxiety, Stress.

172. THE TYPO

A new young monk arrives at the monastery. He is assigned to help the other monks in copying the old canons and laws of the church by hand. He notices, however, that all of the monks are copying from copies, not from the original manuscript. So, the new monk goes to the head abbot to question this, pointing out that if someone made even a small error in the first copy, it would never be picked up. In fact, that error would be continued in all of the subsequent copies.

The head monk, says, "We have been copying from the copies for centuries, but you make a good point, my son."

So, he goes down into the dark caves underneath the monastery where the original manuscript is held as archives in a locked vault that hasn't been opened for hundreds of years. Hours go by and nobody sees the old abbot. So, the young monk gets worried and goes downstairs to look for him. He sees him banging his head against the wall, and wailing "We forgot the "R", we forgot the "R"!"

His forehead is all bloody and bruised and he is crying uncontrollably.

The young monk asks the old abbot, "What's wrong, Father?"

With a choking voice, the old abbot replies:

"The word is celebrate."

* * *

You live in fast spaced society. It is important to stop and smell the roses. Every success is to be celebrated. Celebration serves and supports our human need to be loved and accepted. Celebrate your progress. Look out for good moments, even small and fleeting.

Don't wait until you've reached your goal to be happy with yourself. Be pleased with every step you take toward reaching that goal.

Celebrate your birthdays and anniversaries. Those are occasions to show gratitude to God.

"Celebrations of your accomplishments raise your awareness of what you've done." – Palma Posillico

"The more you praise and celebrate your life, the more there is in life to celebrate." – Oprah Winfrey

Themes: Celebration, Celibate, Festivity, Party, Monk, Religious, Canon, Monastery, Typo, Copy, Manuscript, Abbot.

173. PHOTOGRAPHING WILD FIRES

A photographer from a well-known national magazine was assigned to cover Southern California's wildfires.

The magazine wanted pictures of the heroic work the firefighters were doing as they battled the blazes. When the photographer arrived on the scene, he realized that the smoke was so thick that it would seriously impede, or even make impossible, his obtaining good photographs from ground-level.

He requested permission from his boss to rent a plane and take photos from the air. His request was approved, and via a cell phone call to the local county airport, necessary arrangements were made. He was told a single-engine plane would be waiting for him at the airport.

He arrived at the airfield and spotted a plane warming up outside a hangar. He jumped in with his bag, slammed the door shut, and shouted, "Let's go!"

The pilot taxied out, swung the plane into the wind, and roared down the runway. Within just a minute or two of his arrival they were in the air.

The photographer requested the pilot to, "Fly over the valley and make two or three low passes so I can take some pictures of the fires on the hillsides."

"Why?" asked the pilot.

"Because I'm a photographer for a national magazine," he responded, "and I need to get some close-up shots."

The pilot was strangely silent for a moment; finally he stammered, "So, you're telling me you're not the flight instructor?"

* * *

Things are not always what they seem. Appearance can be deceiving. People and things can look different from the way they truly are. Sometimes people judge based on their past experiences or what the senses perceive.

Remember what the Lord told Samuel: "Do not judge from his appearance or from his lofty stature, because I have rejected him. God does not see as a mortal, who sees the appearance. The Lord looks into the heart." (1 Samuel 16:7)

"If you change the way you look at things, the things you look at change." – Wayne Dyer

Appearance and reality are polar opposites." – Leif Ericsson Leo Veness

Themes: Appearance, Deception, Lord, Judgment, Pilot, Photo, Photographer, Magazine, Instructor.

174. TRAFFIC TICKETS

A man was driving down the road. He passed a traffic camera and saw it flash.

Astounded that he had been caught speeding when he was doing the speed limit, he turned around and, going even slower, he passed by the camera.

Again, he saw it flash. He couldn't believe it! So he turned and, going a snail's pace, he passed the camera.

Again, he saw the camera flash. He guessed it must have a fault, and home he went.

Four weeks later he received 3 traffic fines in the mail, all for not wearing a seat belt.

* * *

Laws are made for man and not man for the laws. When people follow the laws of the land, there is order in the society. Laws regulate society, protect people and solve conflicts. If rules and regulations are broken, you may be liable for punishment. Rules and regulations help keep people safe.

Look at laws, rules, regulations as a help rather than a burden in life. God gave Ten Commandments to the Israelites. Jesus summarized those into two parts: love of God and love of neighbor.

"Blessed are those whose way is blameless, who walk by the law of the Lord." – Psalm 119:1

"Rules only matter if everyone understands them, agrees

to them and can be trusted not to break them. Bearing these irrefutable facts in mind, rules never matter at all." – Seanan McGuire

Themes: Laws, Rules, Regulations, Commandments, Decrees, Traffic, State, Society, Jesus, God.

175. RIDE FOR CHIMPANZEES

A blonde lady motorist was two hours from San Diego, when she was flagged down by a man whose truck had broken down. The man walked up to her car and asked, "Are you going to San Diego?" "Sure," answered the blonde, "do you need a lift?"

"Not for me. I'll be spending the next three hours fixing my truck. My problem is I've got two chimpanzees in the back which have to be delivered to the San Diego Zoo. They're a bit stressed already so I don't want to keep them on the road all day. Could you possibly take them to the zoo for me? I'll give you fifty dollars for your trouble."

"I'd be happy to," said the blonde.

So the two chimpanzees were ushered into the back seat of the blonde's car and carefully strapped into their seat belts. Off they went.

Five hours later, the truck driver was driving through the heart of San Diego when suddenly he was horrified!!

There was the blonde walking down the street and holding hands with the two chimps, much to the amusement of the crowd.

With a screech of brakes he pulled off the road and ran over to the blonde. "What the heck are you doing here?" he demanded, "I gave you fifty dollars to take these chimpanzees to the zoo."

"Yes I know, and I did take them to the zoo" said the blonde, "but we had money left over, so we went to the movies."

* * *

Misunderstanding is caused by faulty communication. Both the sender and receiver are responsible for accurate understanding of the message.

Active listening will help to avoid misunderstanding. Be very specific while communicating. When a communication is not clear, do ask for clarification.

When nails grow long, we cut nails not fingers. Similarly when misunderstandings grow up, cut your ego not your relationship.

"Find the courage to ask questions and to express what you really want. Communicate with others as clearly as you can to avoid misunderstandings, sadness and drama." – Miguel Ruiz

"You never understand a person until you consider things from his point of view." – Harper Lee

Themes: Understanding, Misunderstanding, Communication, Message, Clarification, Question, Relationship, Blonde, Chimpanzee, Zoo, Movies.

176. GNASHING OF TEETH

Grandma told her little grandson: "Be a good boy. At the end of the world all the disobedient and bad will be cast into fiery hell where there will be weeping and gnashing of teeth."

The little boy raised an intelligent doubt. "Grandma, you don't have any teeth and you quarrel with others. How would you gnash your teeth when you are cast into hell?"

Grandma replied: "You naughty boy, don't you know that teeth will be provided."

* * *

We have a provident God who provides for all our needs. God is in complete control of all things. He has a loving care of the humanity. Have total confidence in His benevolence.

Jesus says: "Look at the birds in the sky; they do not sow or reap, they gather nothing into barns, yet your heavenly Father feeds them. Are you not more important than they? Can any of you by worrying add a single moment to your lifespan? Why are you anxious about clothes? Learn from the way the wild flowers grow. They do not work or spin. But I tell you that not even Solomon in all his splendor was clothed like one of them." (Matthew 6: 26-29)

Everything that you have is a gift from God. Be a good steward and be generous with God. God always rewards generosity when you give with the right spirit. He rewards you in every area of your life.

"Sometimes, we need only to look at the sunrise to see the generosity of God." – Jocelyn Soriano

"Sometimes when we are generous in small, barely detectable ways it can change someone else's life forever." – Margret Cho

Themes: God, God's Generosity, Provider, Generosity, Love, Kindness, Confidence, Care, Worry, Anxiety, Steward, Teeth, Boy, Grandma, Grandson.

177. HEARING AID

An elderly gentleman had serious hearing problems for a number of years. He went to the doctor and the doctor was able to have him fitted with a set of hearing aids that allowed the gentleman to hear 100%.

The elderly gentleman went back in a month to the doctor and the doctor said, "Your hearing is perfect. Your family must be really pleased that you can hear again."

The gentleman replied, "Oh, I haven't told my family yet. I just sit around and listen to the conversations. I've changed my will three times!"

* * *

What you will not say in front of someone, do not say behind his or her back. Avoid gossip. It is derogatory conversation about others in their absence. It is betraying trust. Spread no rumor because it can destroy or damage relationships. Remember that if you engage in gossip, others will do the same about you.

People gossip to feel like part of the group, out of envy, out of anger, and to show superiority. It tarnishes the image of other people. God does not want you to listen to gossip either. Be positive in your communication with others and you will build people up.

"How much time he gains who does not look to see what his neighbor says or does or thinks, but only at what he does himself." – Marcus Aurelius

"Great minds discuss ideas. Average minds discuss events. Small minds discuss people." – Eleanor Roosevelt

Themes: Gossip, Rumor, Conversation, Chat, Chat, Hearing Aid, Elderly, Gentleman, Doctor, Family, Will.

178. BREWING THE COFFEE

A man and his wife were having an argument about who should brew the coffee each morning.

The wife said, "You should do it, because you get up first, and then we don't have to wait as long to get our coffee."

The husband said, " You are in charge of cooking around here and you should do it, because that is your job, and I can just wait for my coffee."

Wife replies, "No, you should do it, and besides, it is in the Bible that the man should do the coffee."

Husband replies, "I can't believe that, show me."

So she fetched the Bible, and opened the New Testament

and showed him at the top of several pages, that it indeed says: "HEBREWS".

* * *

Know your Bible. It is our most sacred book which we consider as inspired by God. Bible has two parts: Old Testament and New Testament. "Testament" means "agreement" and "Scripture" means "sacred writings".

Many different authors wrote the Bible over a period of some 1,000 years – from about 900 B.C. to 100 A.D. The Bible is inspired by God.

Read and study the Bible to help you understand God and his works; to know how to live and act; to know about the most famous book in history – the all time best-seller.

"To get the flavor of an herb, it must be pressed between the fingers, so it is the same with the Scriptures; the more familiar they become, the more they reveal their hidden treasures and yield their indescribable riches." – St. John Chrysostom

"When you read God's Word, you must constantly be saying to yourself, 'it is talking to me, and about me.'" – Soren Kierkegaard

Themes: Hebrews, Bible, Bible Study, Word of God, Scriptures, Old Testament, New Testament, Writings, Treasures, Book, Best-seller, Husband, Wife, Argument.

INDEX

(The numbers in index refer to the numbers of the jokes)

Honor, 152

Horse, 43, 169

Hospitality, 147

House, 148

Housekeeper, 111

Housewife, 89

Human, 165

Human Race, 128

Humility, 21,160

Hurt, 83

Husband, 2, 16, 22, 43, 46, 72, 85, 89, 94, 100, 116, 120, 121, 124, 141, 150, 156, 159, 178

Hymns, 44, 90

Hypocritical, 81

IRS, 66

Identity, 23, 60

Ignorance, 132, 139

Imagination, 84

Imitation, 5

Immortality, 14, 80

Incarnation, 26

Industrious, 29

Influence, 38, 170

Ingenuity, 31

Innkeeper, 21

Inspiration, 76

Instructor, 77

Intelligence, 8, 126

Interaction, 72

Interior, 7

Internals, 68

Interpretation, 84

Intimacy, 162

Invention, 31, 54

IPad, 24

Irresponsibility, 139

Israel, 19, 26

Jesuit, 52, 114

Jesus, 5, 13, 19, 24, 27, 29, 44, 93, 113, 114, 156, 174

Jesus Christ, 9, 20, 55, 63, 115, 138, 146, 162

Jewish, 26

Jogging, 37

John the Baptist, 115

Joseph, 21, 114, 156

Joy, 28, 62, 78

Jubilee, 116

Judge, 120

Judgment, 70, 121, 173

Jumping to conclusions, 154

Kid, 114

Kids, 42

Kindness, 33, 62, 147, 176

Knocking, 93

You are welcome to send good jokes or interesting stories for the next volume at <u>HumorToInspiration@gmail.com</u>

Thank you for your valuable time and kindness.

Made in the USA
San Bernardino, CA
20 August 2017